Language in use

BEGINNER

Self-Study Workbook
with answer key

ADRIAN DOFF & CHRISTOPHER JONES

CAMBRIDGE
UNIVERSITY PRESS

PUBLISHED BY THE PRESS SYNDICATE OF THE UNIVERSITY OF CAMBRIDGE
The Pitt Building, Trumping ton Street, cambridge, United Kingdom

CAMBRIDGE UNIVERSITY PRESS
The Edinburgh building, Cambridge, CB2 2RU, UK   www.cup.cam.ac.uk
40 West 20th Street, New York, NY 10011 - 4211, USA   www.cup.org
10 Stamford Road, Oakleigh, Melbourne 3166, Australia
Ruiz de Alarcón 13,, 28014 Madrid, Spain

First Published 1999

Printed in the United Kingdom at the University Press, Cambridge

ISBN 0 521 62705 2   Self-study Workbook with Answer Key
ISBN 0 521 62706 0   Self-study Workbook
ISBN 0 521 62707 9   Classroom Book
ISBN 0 521 62704 4   Teacher's Book
ISBN 0 521 62703 6   Class Cassette Set
ISBN 0 521 62702 8   Self-study Cassette

Contents

To the student

This Workbook contains exercises for you to do on your own.
Like the Classroom Book, it has units and Study Pages.

The units contain:
- homework exercises
- a listening activity
- a list of new words.

The Study Pages contain:
- a progress test
- a phrasebook exercise
- a writing activity.

At the end of the book, there is a Final Review test.

The Workbook has a Self-study Cassette. You will need this for the Listening
exercises in each unit. The tapescipts are at the back of the book.

The Workbook pages look like this:

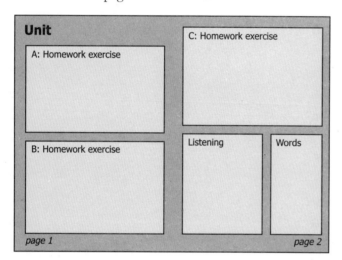

Homework exercises
These give extra practice in the main grammar or
vocabulary of the unit. There are usually three
homework exercises.

Listening
Each unit has a short listening activity.

Words
Some useful vocabulary from the unit. You write
the words in your own language. You can also
add your own words.

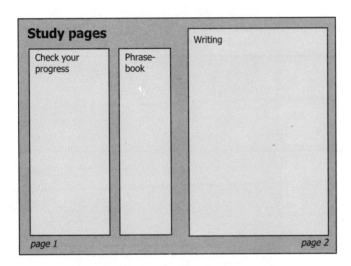

Study pages

Check your progress

Phrase-book

Writing

page 1
page 2

Check your progress
A progress test on the last two units and Study Pages in the Classroom Book.

Phrasebook
This has phrases from the Classroom Book exercise. You write the phrases in your own language.

Writing
Write paragraphs using language from earlier units.

Guide to units

	Self-study Workbook	Classroom Book
1 People and places	**Grammar exercises** Listening: *Photos*	Greetings; introductions; saying where you're from **Grammar:** pronouns; Present tense of *to be*; short forms; *This is ...*
2 In the family	**Vocabulary exercises** Listening: *Parents and children*	Talking about your family; saying how old people are **Vocabulary:** people; family relationships; singular and plural nouns; numbers 1-20
Study pages A	**Check your progress** **Phrasebook** **Writing:** *My friend Maria*	**Focus on ...** The alphabet **Sounds:** /I/, /e/ and /æ/ **Phrasebook:** Greetings **Consolidation:** Pronouns; *have/has; my, your, his, her* **Review**
3 To be or not to be?	**Grammar exercises** Listening: *Spell the words*	Correcting people; asking questions **Grammar:** negative of verb *to be; yes/no* questions; questions with *Who, What* and *Where*
4 Things around you	**Vocabulary exercises** Listening: *Birthday presents*	Describing objects; giving and receiving presents; saying where thing are **Vocabulary:** colours; parts of a room; everday objects; place prepositions
Study pages B	**Check your progress** **Phrasebook** **Writing:** *Pictures of people*	**Focus on ...** Numbers 21-100 **Sounds:** /s/and /θ/, /z/ and /ð/ **Phrasebook:** Excuse me **Consolidation:** *a* and *an; this, that, these, those* **Review**
5 There's...	**Grammar exercises** Listening: *Language school*	Describing and asking about places; finding differences **Grammar:** *These is/are; some* and *any;* questions with *How many ...?*
6 Where you live	**Vocabulary exercises** Listening: *Who are you?*	Talking about flats and houses **Vocabulary:** rooms; furniture; things in the home; addresses and telephone numbers
Study pages B	**Check your progress** **Phrasebook** **Writing:** *Describing places*	**Focus on ...** Possessives **Sounds:** /I/and /i:/ **Phrasebook:** Can I have ...? **Consolidation:** Singular/plural; *a* and *the;* ordinals **Review**

Self-study Workbook		Classroom Book
7 Things people do	**Grammar exercises** Listening: *I like ...*	Saying that people do and don't do **Grammar:** Present simple tense; 3rd person singular; positive and negative forms
8 Food and drink	**Vocabulary exercises** Listening: *In a restaurant*	Saying what you ear and drink; describing dishes; asking for things in restaurant **Vocabulary:** food and drink; things on the table at mealtimes
Study pages D	**Check your progress** **Phrasebook** **Writing:** *Breakfast*	**Focus on ...** Telling the time **Sounds:** /e/, /eɪ/ and /aɪ/ **Phrasebook:** On the phone **Consolidation:** Object pronouns; frequency adverbs **Review**
9 Do you ...?	**Grammar exercises** Listening: *When are they together?*	Asking people about what they do; talking about daily routing **Grammar:** Present simple; *yes/no* questions; *Wh*-questions
10 Things people buy	**Vocabulary exercises** Listening: *Shopping*	Shopping at a marker; talking about shops; saying where shops are **Vocabulary:** buying and selling; shops; things you can buy in shop; place prepositions
Study pages E	**Check your progress** **Phrasebook** **Writing:** *My top three places*	**Focus on ...** Day of the week **Sounds:** /h/ **Phrasebook:** What does it mean? **Consolidation:** Weights and measures; *I like* and *I'd like* **Review**
11 What's going on?	**Grammar exercises** Listening: *On the phone*	Saying what people are doing and where they are; asking what people are doing **Grammar:** Present continuos tense; *yes/no* and *Wh*-questions; place expressions
12 Describing people	**Vocabulary exercises** Listening: *Where are the Browns?*	Saying what people are wearing and what they look like; talking about jobs **Vocabulary:** clothes; job and places of work; adjectives for describing people
Study pages F	**Check your progress** **Phrasebook** **Writing:** *People doing things*	**Focus on ...** Imperatives **Sounds:** /ɒ/ and /ʌ/ **Phrasebook:** Hurry up! **Consolidation:** Expressions *have; at* + place **Review**

	Self-study Workbook	Classroom Book
13 How much?	**Grammar exercises** **Listening:** *I want ...*	Talking and asking about quantity; asking people for things **Grammar:** count and non-count nouns; *much* and *many; some* and *any;* forms of *have got*
14 Around the year	**Vocabulary exercises** **Listening:** *Good times, bad times*	Talking about season, climate and weather **Vocabulary:** words for describing the weather; seasons; months of the year
Study pages G	**Check your progress** **Phrasebook** **Writing:** *Birthdays*	**Focus on ...** Can **Sounds:** /v/ and /w/ **Phrasebook:** Would you like ...? **Consolidation:** *have* and *have got;* numbers over 100; **Review**
15 In the past 1	**Grammar exercises** **Listening:** *The next morning*	Talking about past actions; telling a story; describing something in the past **Grammar:** Past simple tense; Past tense of the verb *to be*; irregular past forms; past time expressions
16 Around the world	**Vocabulary exercises** **Listening:** *Other languages*	Describing countries; talking about languages **Vocabulary:** geographical terms; names of countries and continents; languages
Study pages H	**Check your progress** **Phrasebook** **Writing:** *and, so, because*	**Focus on ...** Dates **Sounds:** /ʃ/, /tʃ/ and /dʒ/ **Phrasebook:** I'm not sure **Consolidation:** Verbs with to objects; *in* and *on* + place **Review**
17 In the past 2	**Grammar exercises** **Listening:** Can you remember?	Saying what people did and didn't do: asking questions about the past; remembering **Grammar:** Past simple tense, positive and negative; *yes/no* and *Wh*-questions; more irregular past forms
18 How to get there	**Vocabulary exercises** **Listening:** Bags of gold	Talking about ways of traveling and moving around; giving directions **Vocabulary:** direction prepositions; public transport; expressions for giving directions
Study pages I	**Check your progress** **Phrasebook** **Writing:** *Then ...*	**Focus on ...** Short answers **Sounds:** /l/ **Phrasebook:** Let's ... **Consolidation:** *very, quite* and *not very;* years **Review**

	Classroom Book	Self-study Workbook
Unit19 You mustn't dot that	**Grammar exercises** **Listening:** *House rules*	Explaining rules; asking for and giving permission; saying what you have to and don't have to do **Grammar:** *must* and *mustn't; can* and *can't; have to* and *don't have to*
Unit20 The body	**Vocabulary exercises** **Listening:** *Exercises*	Describing bodies and actions; describing physical appearance; describing actions **Vocabulary:** parts of the body; adjectives describing physical appearance ; action verbs
Study pages J	**Check your progress** **Phrasebook** **Writing:** *Animals*	**Focus on ...** Adverbs **Sounds:** /r/ **Phrasebook:** Could you ... ? **Consolidation:** Verb with *to, at* and *about* **Review**
Unit21 Good, better, best	**Grammar exercises** **Listening:** *Buying things*	Making comparisons; describing outstanding features **Grammar:** comparative adjectives; *than;* superlative adjectives
Unit22 Free time	**Vocabulary exercises** **Listening:** *At the weekend*	Talking about leisure activities and sport; talking about likes and dislikes **Vocabulary:** leisure facilities activities and sports; leisure facilities; *like/enjoy* + -ing
Study pages K	**Check your progress** **Phrasebook** **Writing:** *and, but, also*	**Focus on ...** Verb + *to* + infinitive **Sounds:** /aː/, /ɔː/, /ɜː/ and /ə/ **Phrasebook:** What did you say? **Consolidation:** Expressions with *go* **Review**
Unit23 Future plans	**Grammar exercises** **Listening:** *At the airport*	Talking and asking questions about future plans; talking about future arrangements **Grammar:** *going to;* questions with *going to;* Present continuous tense with future meaning
Unit24 Feelings	**Vocabulary exercises** **Listening:** *Three stories*	Describing feeling; expressing opinions about films and TV programmes **Vocabulary:** physical feeling; emotions; adjectives describing quality
Final review		

1 People and places

A Hello and goodbye

Match the people. Write the conversations.

1 - Hello, I'm Isabelle
  - Oh, hi. My name's Joe.

2 - ....
  - ....

3 - ....
  - ....

4 - ....
  - ....

5 - ....
  - ....

B To be

1 Complete the table.

to be	
Long form	*Short form*
I am	I'm
....	You're
....	He's
She is	....
....	It's
....	We're
They are	....

2 Fill the gaps in the bubbles.
Use short forms.

This is Carlos. .... from Granada.

This is Brazil. .... very big

This is Helen. .... from London.

This is Jack and this is Carol. .... from New York.

Hi. I'm Jill and this is Peter. .... teachers here.

C Countries

Complete these sentences. Write countries in the diagram.

1 Paris and Marseilles are in ... ➤
2 Moscow and St Petersburg are in ... ➤
3 Madrid and Barcelona are in ... ➤
4 London and Edinburgh are in ... ➤
5 Berlin and Munich are in ... ➤
6 Tokyo and Osaka are in ... ➤
7 Rome and Bologna are in ... ➤
8 Rio de Janairo and São Paolo are in ... ➤
9 Washington and New York are in the ... ➤

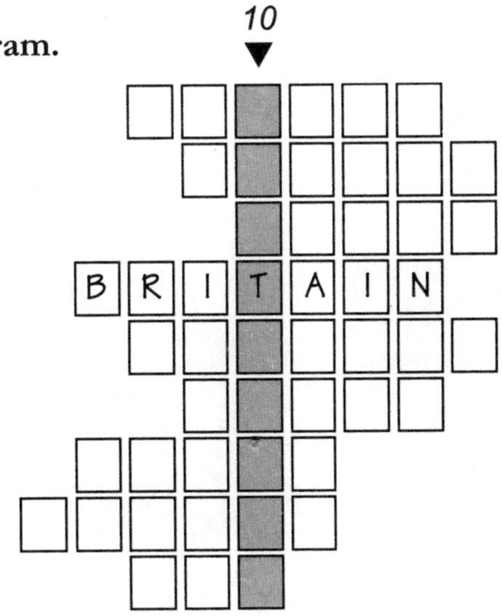

What is country number 10?

10

B R I T A I N

Listening: Photos

Listen and complete the sentences.

1 This is my friend Julia. She's ....
....
....

2 This is my flat in London. It's ....
....
It's ....

3 This is John. He's ....
....and
....

4 This is my car. It's ....
but ....
....

5 These are my friends Bill and
Graham. They're ....
....

Words

Write these words in your language.

teacher ....
student ....
friend ....
flat ....
house ....
room ....
car ....
big ....
small ....
new ....
old ....
I think ....
I don't know ....

Other words

....
....
....
....
....

2 In the family

A One baby, two houses...

What can you see? Write under the pictures.

one baby

two houses

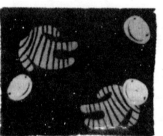

....

....

....

....

....

....

....

Singular and plural
To make a plural, add -*s*:

a boy	→	boys
a bird	→	birds
a car	→	cars

-*y* changes to -*ies*:

a baby	→	babies
a family	→	families

Note:

a child	→	children

B Numbers 1-20

1 Write the missing numbers in the table.

2 What are the answers?

a six + seven + two = ...

b three + one + nine = ...

c eight + four + seven = ...

d ten + four + six = ...

e three + four + five = ...

f five + six + seven = ...

g four + six + one = ...

11	eleven
12	
13	
14	
15	
16	
17	
18	
19	
20	

C The family

1 Write the missing words in the boxes.

| wife | ⟷ | |

daughter ⟷ [ ]

father ⟷ [ ]

[ ] ⟷ brother

2 Write about your family.

I have ....

....

Listening: *Parents and children*

1 🔲 Listen and choose the correct picture.

1 .... 2 .... 3 .... 4 ....

Words

Write these words in your language.

child	....
children	....
family	....
parents	....
married	....
doctor	....
taxi driver	....
university	....
birthday	....

Other words

....	....
....	....
....	....
....	....
....	....
....	....

2 How old are they? Listen again and write numbers in the boxes.

Check your progress

1 **Write the missing letters.**

(green) B C .... G .... T V

(red) .... M .... S X

(grey) A ....

(blue) Q ....

(white) I ....

D	L
E	N
F	P
J	U
K	Y

2 **Fill the gaps.**

I'm	He's	She's	It's	They're

a This is my friend Peter. .... from Australia.

b I have three dogs. .... very big!

c Hello. .... Nadia. What's your name?

d My sister is 19. .... a student.

e This is my old TV. .... black and white.

3 **Fill the gaps. with** *have or has*.

a He .... black hair.

b Alex and Joanna .... four children.

c I .... blue eyes, but my sister .... green eyes.

d Her parents .... a green Mercedes.

4 **Write these numbers.**

5 ....   14 ....

7 ....   18 ....

12 ....   20 ....

5 **Write one word in each gap.**

a I'm her father. She's my ....

b I'm her husband. She's my ....

c I'm his father. He's my ....

d We have three .... - two girls and a boy.

e We have one .... He's a boy.

Phrasebook

Write these conversations in your language.

Good morning.

....

Good afternoon.

....

Good evening, sir.

Good evening.

....

....

R E S   Good night.   R   A   N   T

....

Writing: *My friend Maria*

1 Look at the notes. Then read the paragraph.

Notes

<u>My friend Maria</u>

from Madrid in Spain
18 years old
a student
black hair, brown eyes
and small car

Paragraph

My friend Maria *is* from Madrid in Spain. *She's* 18 years old *and she's* a student. *She has* black hair *and* brown eyes. *She has* a small car

2 Write a paragraph from the notes.

Notes

<u>My brother Ed</u>
6 years old
brown hair, grey eyes
a green bike

Paragraph

....
....
....
....

3 Write about one friend, and one person in your family.

a ....
....
....
....

b ....
....
....
....

3 To be or not to be?

A I'm not...

Complete the sentences. Use short forms in your answers.

1 I .... from England - I'm from Scotland.

2 She .... my wife - she's my sister.

3 You .... in Class 2A - you're in class 2B.

4 My friends .... from the USA. They're from Canada.

5 His house .... big - it's small.

6 We .... teachers - we're students.

7 I .... eighteen. I'm only sixteen.

8 That .... a dog - it's a cat.

to be - negative forms	
Long form	*Short form*
I am not	I'm not
You are not	You aren't
He/she is not	He/she isn't
We are not	We aren't
You are not	You aren't
They are not	They aren't

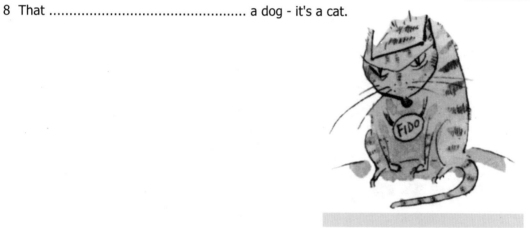

B Yes/no questions

Look at these examples.

I think he's Peter Brown.
.. Is he Peter Brown? ....

I think they're married.
.. Are they married? ....

Yes/no questions	
He is Peter Brown.	They're married.
Is he Peter Brown?	Are they married?

Ask *yes/no* questions.

1 I think he's English. ....

2 I think you're a doctor. ....

3 I think she's from California. ....

4 I think this is your car. ....

5 I think it's your birthday. ....

6 I think your name is Chris. ....

7 I think you're a policeman. ....

C Wh- questions

Here are some answers.
What are the questions? Use the table.

1 - ....

  - I'm fine, thanks.

2 - ....

  - He's seventeen.

3 - ....

  - They're my parents.

4 - ....

  - It's Alice Brown.

5 - ....

  - It's in Italy.

Who		Rome?
What	is	you?
Where		her name?
How	are	your brother?
How old		these people?

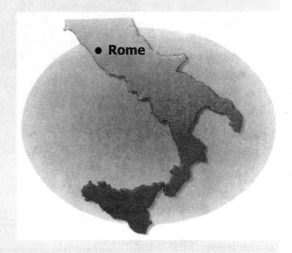

● Rome

Listening: *Spell the words*

The words in this picture are new.
Listen and write them down.

1 ....

2 ....

3 ....

4 ....

5 ....

6 ....

7 ....

Words

Write these words in your language.

waiter   ....

customer   ....

a cup of coffee ....

Happy birthday! ....

seat   ....

free   ....

banana ·   ....

book   ....

person   ....

people   ....

Other words

....

....

....

....

....

....

....

4 Things around you

A Colours

Can you remember the colours?

Complete the sentences. Then look at the picture in the Classroom Book (page 19).

1 The sky *is blue.* ....

2 The trees *are green and black.* ....

3 The chair ....

4 The floor ....

5 The hair ....

6 The face ....

7 The book ....

8 The dress ....

9 The table ....

10 The wall ....

11 The shoes ....

12 The door ....

B Things

There are 18 things in the picture. Can you find them in the wordsquare?

U	B	J	D	O	O	R	E
M	O	U	N	T	A	I	N
B	O	M	X	A	A	N	F
R	K	P	L	B	R	G	O
E	P	E	N	L	S	K	O
L	T	R	E	E	H	C	T
L	W	I	N	D	O	W	B
A	A	C	A	M	E	R	A
B	T	D	R	E	S	S	L
A	C	H	A	I	R	T	L
G	H	T	L	A	M	P	Q

C It's on the desk

Use the table to answer these questions.

1 Where's the football?

....

2 Where are the shoes?

....

3 Where are the books?

....

4 Where's the bike?

....

5 Where are the glasses?

....

6 Where's the dog?

....

	on	the window.
It's	by	the chair.
	under	the desk.
They're	in	the door.
	behind	the bag.

Listening: *Birthday presents*

🔊 Seven people talk about their birthday presents.
Listen and write numbers by the pictures.

Three pictures have no number. Which are they?

....

Words

Write these words in your language.

face   ....

hair   ....

CD   ....

address book ....

glasses   ....

computer   ....

desk   ....

wall   ....

floor   ....

Other words

....

....

....

....

....

....

Check your progress

1 Write these numbers.

30 .... 47 ....

62 ....

2 What are these things? Use *a* or *an*.

.a chair........... ....

....

....

....

3 Fill the gaps with *this, these, that* or *those*.

.... are nice houses.

Is............. your car?

..............is my son Sam.

4 Fill the gaps with *is, isn't, are* or *aren't*.

a Rubies .... red. Emeralds .... red.

b Edinburgh .... in France. Paris and Marseilles

.... in France.

c Where .... my pen? Where .... my books?

5 What colour are these boxes?

■ .... □ .... ■ ....

Write the names of *five* other colours.

....

....

6 Look at the picture, and fill the gaps.

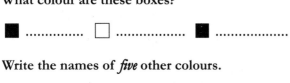

a The bag is .... the chair.

b The ball is .... the chair.

c The book is .... the bag.

d The chair is .... the door.

Phrasebook

Write these conversations in your language.

Oh, sorry.

That's all right

....

....

Excuse me. Mr Brown's on the phone.

OK. Excuse me. just a moment.

....

....

....

....

Excuse me ... Excuse me!

Oh, sorry

....

....

Writing: *Pictures of people*

1 Look at the notes. Then read the paragraph.

Notes

me with my baby
Louisa
one year old
in my flat in Paris

Paragraph

This is a picture of me with my baby.
Her name is Louisa, *and she's* one year old.
We're in my flat in Paris.

2 Write paragraphs from the notes.

Notes

me with my girlfriend
Carla
from the USA
on holiday in Spain

Paragraph

This is a picture of ....
....
....
....
....

Notes

me with my parents
my father: 50
my mother: 40
in their house in London

Paragraph

This is ....
....
....
....

3 Add your own picture. Write about it.

This is ....
....
....
....
....
....

5 There's...

A There is and there are

Say what there is in the picture.
Use *There is* (or *There's*) and *There are*.

....
....
....
....
....
....
....
....
....
....
....

B In my town...

Read the examples in the box.
Write true sentences about your town.

In my town ...	
... there's an airport.	... there are some beautiful beaches.
... there isn't and university.	... there are three swimming pools.
... there are lost of shops.	... there aren't any good restaurants.
... there are some hotels.	... there aren't any churches.

In my town
....
....
....
....
....
....

C Asking questions

Use the words to make questions

1 beaches here any there near are good?
   Are there any good beaches near here?
   ....

2 a town there good in is this restaurant?

   ....

3 this in floors building many there how are?

   ....

4 people many how your in there are family?

   ....

5 your in university is town there a?

   ....

6 many exercise questions are this there in how?

   ....

Listening: *Language school*

Read this text about a language school.

The English Language Centre has about 500 students and 20 teachers. There are about 10-15 students in each class.

The school is on two floors. There are six class-rooms. There isn't a café for the students, but there is a coffee machine. There is also a small library - it has about 100 books. There aren't any computers at the school, but there is a video in each classroom.

Now listen to the conversation. Find five things that are different from the text.

1 ....

2 ....

3 ....

4 ....

5 ....

Words

Write these words in your language.

place   ....

shop   ....

tourist   ....

building   ....

swimming pool....................................

stairs   ....

lift   ....

toilet   ....

favourite   ....

beautiful   ....

Other words

....

....

....

....

....

....

A Things in the home

What is there in these rooms? Write numbers in the boxes.

14	bath
8	bed
	carpet
	clock
	cooker
	cupboard
	fridge
	mirror
	phone
	picture
	plant
	radio
	shelf
	shower
	sofa
	television

B Where are they?

Look at the rooms again and complete these sentences.

1 There's a clock ..... *in the bedroom, on the table by the bed.* .....

2 There's a phone ....

3 There's a picture ....

4 There's a plant ....

5 There's a radio ....

6 There's a mirror ....

7 There's a television ....

There's a (clock)...	
... in	the living room the bedroom the bathroom the kitchen
... in the corner	
... on	the fridge the wall the shelf the table
... by	the window the door the bed the sofa

C Names and addresses

Look at these two cards, and fill the gaps.

1 The man is a ......<u>taxi driver</u>...... and the woman is the .... of a language school.

2 The woman's last name is .... and the man's first name is ....

3 The language school is in a street called ...., and its phone number is ....

4 The man's city is ...., which is in .... His post code is ....

PORTOBELLO TAXIS

Paul Richardson,
10 Bath Street,
Edinburgh EH15 3TW,
Scotland.
☎ 0131 024901

Villa Rosa
SCHOOL OF ENGLISH

Lisa Morelli (Director)
Via Napoli 192
19840 Rome
Italy
☎ 0112394023

Listening: *Who are you?*

Listen and complete the form.

NAME: ....

ADDRESS: ....

....

....

TELEPHONE: ....

Words

Write these words in your language.

single bed ....

double bed ....

hall ....

balcony ....

plan ....

of course ....

in the corner ....

address ....

Other words

....

....

....

....

....

....

....

....

....

Check your progress

1 Fill the gaps.

(I)   I'm Tony and this is ......my...... brother Leo.

(you)   Excuse me. Is this .... umbrella?

(he)   Micheal's here. That's .... bike.

(she)   This is my sister with .... dog, Gigi.

(we)   That's .... new car over there.

(they)   They have a TV in .... bedroom.

(Ronaldo) Is that .... football?

2 Make these words plural.

girl ....   beach ....

baby ....   table ....

glass ....   carpet ....

3 These numbers are in a lift. Which floors are they?

2 ..the second floor.....   **6** ....

3 ....   **8** ....

4 Look at the room and complete the sentences.

a There .... fridge in the room.

b There .... shower.

c There .... cupboards.

d There .... plants.

Now complete these sentences.

e There's .... in the corner.

f There's .... on the shelf.

g There's .... on the wall.

Phrasebook

Write these conversations in your language.

Can I have a glass of orange juice?

Yes, of course.

....

....

....

Can I have a glass of water, please?

Yes, here you are.

....

....

....

Can I have a cup of coffee, please?

Certainly, sir.

....

....

....

Writing: *Describing places*

1 **Look at these examples.**

Our hotel's very good.
The rooms are big.
It's right by the sea.

Our hotel's very good.
The rooms are big, *and*
It's right by the sea.

Our hotel is OK.
It isn't by the sea.
There's a swimming pool.

Our hotel is OK. It isn't
by the sea, *but there's a*
swimming pool.

2 **Choose sentences from the box. Join them with** *and or but.*

a Our village is very small. ....

   ....

   ....

b My hotel room is OK. ....

   ....

   ....

c Their house is fantastic. ....

   ....

   ....

There isn't a school.
The bed's very comfortable.
There's a swimming pool in the garden.
There isn't a TV.
There's only one shop.
There are eight bedrooms.

3 **Write about one of these things.**

A hotel or flat	A hotel	A school	A town or village	A room

....

....

....

....

7 Things people do

A Verbs

Write verbs in the gaps.

go	~~listen~~	play	talk
have	look	read	watch

1 ....listen........... to music
   to the radio

2 .... a newspaper
   a magazine

3 .... out of the window

4 .... a sandwich
   a burger
   football

5 .... a computer game
   cards

6 .... television
   a video

7 .... to my friends

8 .... to the shops
   to the park

B I speak- She speaks

I You We They	speak English.	He She My mother Louis	speaks English.

Fill the gaps. Use the verbs in the boxes.

1 | speak/speaks | I'm from America. I .... English and Spanish

My husband is French, and he .... French and Spanish.

At home, we .... Spanish.

2 | have/has | My friend Joe usually .... a burger at lunchtime.

Sometimes he .... two burgers. I usually .... a sandwich.

3 | like/likes | My sister .... white coffee, and my brother

.... black coffee. I .... black coffee and white coffee.

4 | play/plays | My parents .... tennis. My mother also ....

table tennis. I just .... football.

C Adjectives

Here are six pairs of opposites. Write the answers in the crossword.

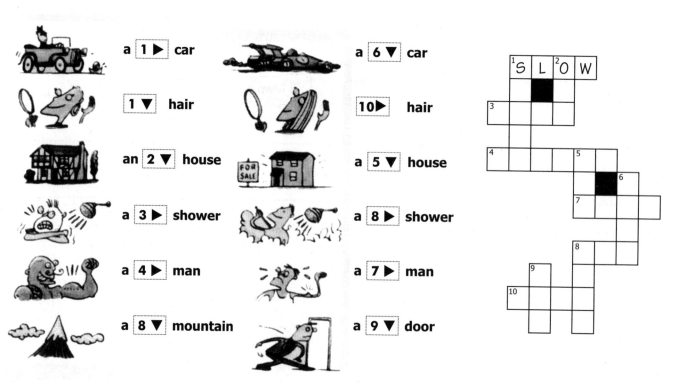

a 1 ▶ car   a 6 ▼ car

1 ▼ hair   10▶ hair

an 2 ▼ house   a 5 ▼ house

a 3 ▶ shower   a 8 ▶ shower

a 4 ▶ man   a 7 ▶ man

a 8 ▼ mountain   a 9 ▼ door

D Positive and negative

Make these sentences negative.

I			He		
You			She		
We	**don't** speak *English*.		My mother	**doesn't** speak *English*.	
They			Louis		

Examples:

My father speaks English   →   My father doesn't speak English.

Birds drink coffee.   →   Birds don't drink coffee.

a His parents speak Chinese. → ....

b She wears beautiful clothes. → ....

c My mother likes beer. → ....

d I live in Los Angeles. → ....

e John goes to a good school. → ....

f My children play football. → ....

g My dog watches TV. → ....

Listening: *I like ...*

🔊 **Listen to Marianne.**

1 Which sentences are true, and which are false? Write *T* or *F*.

a ☐ She likes Italian food.

b ☐ She doesn't drink beer or wine.

c ☐ She drinks a lot of coffee.

d ☐ She often drinks water.

e ☐ She plays music at home.

f ☐ She likes black clothes.

g ☐ She's from France.

h ☐ She speaks French and English.

2 Write two other true sentences about her.

a She likes ....

b She doesn't like ....

Words

Write these words in your language.

sometimes	....
usually	....
sleep (v.)	....
ill	....
clothes	....
Why?	....
because	....
meat	....
tennis	....
piano	....
smoke (v.)	....
Other words	
....	....
....	....
....	....
....	....
....	....
....	....

8 Food and drink

A Types of food

Do you remember these pictures?
What types of food do they show?

1

2

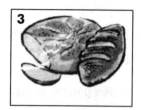
3

..... Vegetables .....

....

....

4

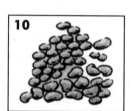
5

6

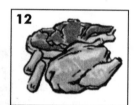
7

8

....

....

....

....

....

9

10

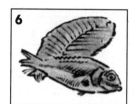
11

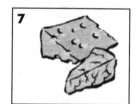
12

13

....

....

....

....

....

B I drink ...

Read the examples. Then write about yourself. You can
use the drinks in the list, and any others you want.

On a hot day, I like a glass of lemonade or beer.

With my breakfast, I usually drink coffee.
Sometimes I have fruit juice.

I don't drink milk.

a With my breakfast, ...	water
b With my lunch, ...	milk
c With my dinner, ...	tea
d When I'm at a party, ...	coffee
e On a hot day, ...	fruit juice
f On a cold day, ...	lemonade
g My favourite drink is	Coca-Cola
h I never drink	beer
	wine
	....
	....

C Where are they?

What are these things? Write them in the puzzle.

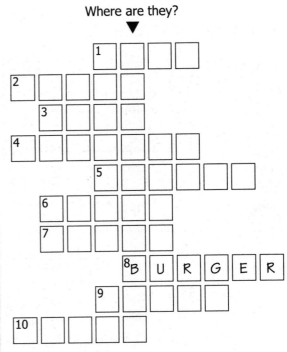

Where are they? ▼

8. B U R G E R

Now read the answer to the question *Where are they ?*

Listening: *In a restaurant*

Listen to the conversations and complete the sentences.

Conversation 1

The woman has ....
....
....
....
The man has ....
....
....
....

Conversation 2

The man wants ....
....
The man has ....
....

Chicken with potatoes
Fish with rice
Meatballs with rice
Spaghetti bolognese
Vegetables
Green salad
Tomato salad

DRINKS
Coca-Cola
Lemonade
Orange juice
Beer

Words

Write these words in your language.

a glass of milk ....
a milk shake ....
every day ....
usually ....
often ....
sometimes ....
never ....
I'm very sorry ....
Yes, of course ....

Other words

....
....
....
....
....

D Study pages

Check your progress

1 What time is it?

....

....

....

....

2 Fill the gaps.

(I) Excuse ...me........!

(he) John's my friend. I like ....

(she) She talks a lot, but I never listen to ....

(we) Our daughter visits .... on Sundays.

(they) I don't eat apples. I don't like ....

3 Fill the gaps. Use verbs from the box.

| go | have | listen | read | watch |

In the morning...

a ... my parents .... to the radio.

b ... my mother .... a shower.

c ... my father .... the newspaper.

d ... I .... the news on TV.

e ... my brother .... to school.

f ... my parents .... to work.

4 Look at the table and complete the sentences. Use the verb *eat*.

a Jim and Sue .... fish.

b They .... cheese.

c Jim .... eggs.

d Sue .... eggs.

	Jim	Sue
fish	✓	✓
cheese	X	X
eggs	X	✓

Phrasebook

Write these conversations in your language.

Hello. Is Mr. Black there, please?
No he isn't. Sorry.
OK. Never mind.

....
....
....
....

Hello. Can I speak to Mr Black, please?
Yes. Just a moment.

....
....
....
....

Hello. Dave Black.
Hello, Dave. It's Paula.
Oh, hi, Paula.

....
....
....
....

Writing: *Breakfast*

1 Look at the picture. Then read the paragraph.

toast

butter

jam

(eggs)

milk

I *have* breakfast at about haft past eight.
I *usually have* toast with butter and jam, and I
sometimes have eggs. And *I drink* a glass of milk.

2 Write about these breakfasts.

bread

cheese

(fruit)

orange juice

I have breakfast at ....
....
....
....
....
....

rolls

cheese

cold meat

(jam)

coffee

I have breakfast at ....
....
....
....
....
....

3 Now write about your breakfast.

I have breakfast at ....
....
....
....
....

9 Do you ...?

A Yes/no questions.

Look at these examples.

Do you		
Do they		like chocolate?
Does he		
Does she		

I think you play tennis.   →   *Do you play tennis?*

I think your brother likes tea.   →   *Does your brother like tea?*

Ask yes/no questions

1 I think your parents smoke. ....

2 I think she eats burgers. ....

3 I think he lives in California. ....

4 I think you have sugar in your coffee. ....

5 I think your children like pasta. ....

6 I think she drives a Mercedes. ....

7 I think your friends live near here. ....

B Wh-questions

Kasia answers questions about herself and her family. Read about her, then write the missing questions.

Kasia is from Poland. Her parents live in Warsaw, but she lives in London. She studies maths at London University.

Kasia has a brother and a sister. Her sister lives in Vienna, and works in a bank. Her brother lives with her parents in Warsaw. He studies French and English at Warsaw University.

1 - *Where do your parents live?* ....

  - In Warsaw.

2 - *Where do you live?* ....

  - In London.

3 - ....

  - Maths.

4 - ....

  - At London University.

5 - *Where does your sister live?* ....

  - In Vienna.

6 - ....

  - In a bank.

7 - ....

  - With my parents in Warsaw.

8 - ....

  - French and English.

9 - ....

  - At Warsaw University.

C Daily routine

Write sentences about your daily routine. Use the questions to help you.

> What time do you get up?

> What time do you have breakfast?

> What time do you go to work/school?

> What time do you star work/school?

> What time do you have lunch?

> What time do you finish work/school?

> What time do you come home?

> What time do you have dinner?

> What time do you go to bed?

I usually get up at

....

....

....

....

....

....

....

Listening: *When are they together?*

A married couple talk about their daily routine.

1  **Listen and write times in the gaps.**

The man works for a 24-hour radio station. He goes to work at .... in the evening and gets home at .... in the morning Then he goes to bed. He gets up at .... and has lunch. Then he watches TV or reads He has dinner at ...., and then it's time to go to work again.

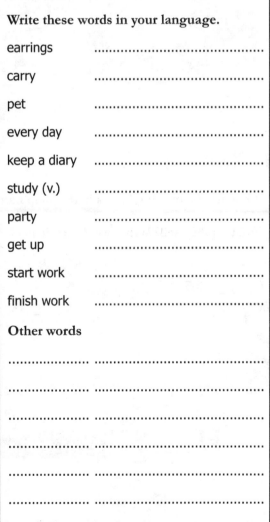

The woman works in a supermarket. She gets up at .... in the morning, has breakfast and goes to work. She gets home from work at .... in the evening and has dinner at about .... Then she watches TV or reads, and she goes to bed at about ....

2 **When do they have time together?**

From .... to ....

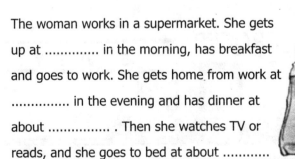

Words

Write these words in your language.

earrings	....
carry	....
pet	....
every day	....
keep a diary	....
study (v.)	....
party	....
get up	....
start work	....
finish work	....

Other words

....

....

....

....

....

....

....

10 Things people buy

A Customers

What are the customers saying?
Make sentences from the table
and write them in the bubbles.

How much is	that football?
How much are	this jacket?
That's	that camera?
I'll have	~~those shoes?~~
Can I see	these jeans?
What size is	too expensive!
~~What size are~~	five, please.

1 What size are those shoes? / They're size 52.

2 It's £9.50.

3 Yes of course. Here you are.

4 It's size 29.

5 OK. That's £2.50, please

6 They're £30.

7 This is a nice one. Only £150.

B Shops

1 What are the missing letters in the shop names? Write them in.

2 What do they sell? Write two things in each shop.

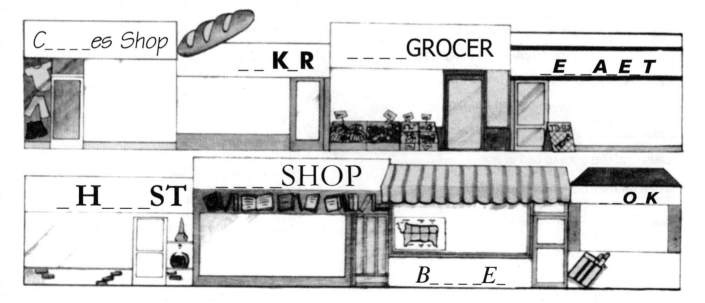

C_____es Shop

_ _ K_R

_ _ _ _ _ GROCER

_E_ _A_E_T

_H_ _ _ST

_ _ _ _ _ SHOP

_ _ O_K

B_ _ _ _E_

C Where is it?

Write prepositions in the gaps.

in	by	near	next to
between	opposite		

1 The restaurant is ....
   Washington Street, just
   .... the cinema.

2 The supermarket is
   .... the cinema.

3 The post office is ....
   the park.

4 The petrol station is
   .... Queen Street,
   .... the river.

5 The bank is .... the petrol
   station and the station.

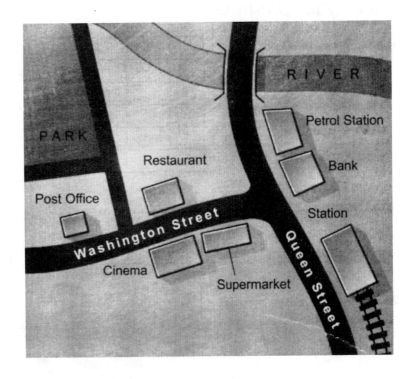

Listening: *Shopping*

Listen to the three conversations.
Where are the people? What do they buy?

1 Shop: ....
   She buys: ....
   ....
   ....

2 Shop: ....
   She buys: ....
   ....

3 Shop: ....
   She buys: ....
   She doesn't buy: ....

Words

Write these words in your language.

Can I help you?	....
expensive	....
too big	....
It's open	....
It's closed	....
open (v.)	....
close (v.)	....
all night	....
until	....

Other words

....	....
....	....
....	....
....	....
....	....

Check your progress

1 Look at the table and complete the sentences.

	9-12	2-5	7-9
M	shower		
T		tennis	
W			cards
T	shops		
F			cinema

John Smith has a shower.
...on Monday morning... .

He plays tennis ....

.... and

he plays cards ....

He goes to the shops .... and

he goes to the cinema ....

2 What does the customer say?

Good morning. I'd like...

3 KG POTATOES	*three* ....
1/2 KG SUGAR	....
1/2 L MILK	*and* .... *please* ....

3 Make questions using these words.

a up you do time get what?

....

b are size shoes what those?

....

c live parents where your do?

....

d how is radio much this?

....

e brother does study what your?

....

4 Look at the plan. Which shop is:

a opposite the bank? ....

b next to the hotel? ....

c between the bank and the post office? ....

d opposite the greengrocer? ....

Phrasebook

Write these questions in your language.

What does 'vegetable' mean?

....

....

What's 'merci' in English?

....

....

Writing: *My top three places*

1 A man writes about shops and cafés in his town.

	1 C & A
O	C & A is a big clothes shop. It stays open till seven in the evening, but it's closed on Sunday. The clothes there are good and they aren't very expensive. I often buy jeans, jumpers and T-shirt there.

	2 Green Street Market
O	This is a very big market. It's open on Saturday and Sunday morning. You can buy everything there - furniture, flowers, clothes, things for the kitchen, pictures, old
O	book, gold rings . . . I usually go there on Saturdays.

	3 The Food Factory
	This is a restaurant and a café. They sell soup, burgers, and salads. You can also have just a drink. It's open from ten in the morning till six in the evening.
O	I sometimes go there on Saturday with my friends.

2 What are your top three places?

1 ....
....
....

2 ....
....
....

3 ....
....
....

Useful expressions
This is a ...
They sell ...
You can buy ... there
It's open from ... to ...
It stays open till ...
I often go there ...
I usually buy ...

11 What's going on?

A They're listening to the radio

Complete the table. Then say what the people are doing.

Verb	Verb + -ing
drink	drinking
listen	....
play	....
read	....
wash	....
watch	....
dance	dancing
have	....
make	....
write	....

1

They're listening
to the radio

2

She's watching
television.

3

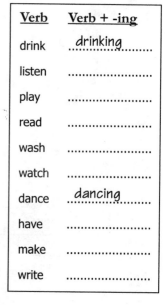

....

4

....

....

5

....

....

6

....

....

7

....

....

8

....

....

9

....

....

10

....

....

B Asking questions

Write questions with *What* and *Where*.

What	are you	
	are they	... ing?
Where	is he	
	is she	

1 Is she reading a newspaper / *a book?*

What is she reading? ....

2 Are you staying with friends / *at a hotel?*

....

3 Are they watching a film / *a football match?*

....

4 Is he drinking lemonade / *a milk shake?*

....

5 Are you going to the shops / *to a friend's house?*

....

6 Are they playing cards / *a computer game*

....

7 Is she working at home / *at school?*

....

C Where is he?

The photos show a boy in seven different places. Where is he in each one? Choose from the table.

	home
	school
	the cinema
at	the swimming pool
	the shops
	the post office
	a party

1

at the swimming pool.

2

....

3

....

4

....

5

....

6

....

7

....

Listening: *On the phone*

Listen to the conversations.
Answer these questions about each person.

A Is he/she at home?

B What is he/she doing?

C Can he/she come to the phone?

1 Ali

A ....

B ....

....

....

C ....

2 Sam

A ....

B ....

....

....

C ....

3 Susie

A ....

B ....

....

....

C ....

4 Mrs Lopez

A ....

B ....

....

....

C ....

Words

Write these words in your language.

do your
homework ....

sit ....

football match ....

(They're) out ....

(She's) away ....

(He's) asleep ....

I'm afraid ....

chess ....

Other words

....

....

....

....

A Clothes

1 What are these clothes in English?
The answers are all in the wordsquare.

S	H	I	R	T	O	S	I
J	A	C	K	E	T	H	L
A	T	C	J	N	J	O	T
T	R	O	U	S	E	R	S
I	D	A	M	W	A	T	H
E	X	T	P	U	N	S	I
O	D	R	E	S	S	J	R
S	K	I	R	T	U	P	T
S	U	S	U	I	T	J	E

2 What clothes are you wearing? What colour are they?
I'm wearing ....
....

B Jobs

Write about these people.

	a doctor.			teaches maths.
	an engineer.			studies French.
He's	a secretary.		He	works for an electricity company.
	a shop assistant.			works for British Airways.
She's	a student.		She	works in a hospital.
	a teacher.			works in a French restaurant.
	a waiter.			works in a newsagent.

1

He's an engineer.
He works for an
electricity company.

2 ....
....
....

3 ....
....
....

4 ....
....

5 ....
....
....

6 ....
....

7 ....
....
....

C In the family

Write about two people in your family. Use the questions to help you.

> How old are they?

> Are they tall? short?

> Do they have long hair? short hair? fair hair? dark hair?

> Do they wear glasses?

> What clothes do they usually wear?

1 My...

....

....

....

....

> Do they have children? How many?

2 ....

....

....

....

....

> Do they drive a car? What kind?

> Do they have jobs? Where do they work?

Listening: *Where are the Browns?*

You're looking for three people at a party: Mr Brown, Mrs Brown and their son Richard.

Listen and find them in the picture.

Person .... is Mr Brown.   Person .... is Mrs Brown.

Person .... is Richard.

Words

Write these words in your language.

French   ....

band   ....

driver (a car) ....

hospital   ....

insurance   ....

company   ....

song   ....

builder   ....

busy   ....

love   ....

Other words

....

....

....

....

Check your progress

1 Fill the gaps with imperatives.
Choose from the box.

buy	don't buy
close	don't close
look	don't look
open	don't open
play	don't play
read	don't read

a .... your

books and ....

story on page 25.

b .... the

window, please. It's cold.

c .... the piano! The children are asleep.

d .... at that man's hair- it's green!

e .... that jacket. It's too expensive.

2 What are you doing (and not doing) now?
Write true sentences using the Present continuous tense.

(wear) *I'm wearing* ....

(write) ....

(sit) ....

(not wear) *I'm not wearing* ....

(not play) ....

(not have) ....

3 What are these people's jobs?

....

Write the names of four other jobs.

....

....

4 Describe this person. What is he wearing?

....

....

....

....

....

Phrasebook

Write these expressions in your language.

Hurry up!

....

Sit down!

....

Wait a minute.

....

Come in!

....

Be quiet!

....

Writing: *People doing things*

1 Look at the notes. Then read the paragraph.

Notes

a girl, a boy

the girl: a dress

the boy: shorts, a
T. shirt

looking out of the
window

in the street: a police car

Paragraph

The picture shows a girl and a boy. The girl is
wearing a dress, and the boy is wearing shorts and a
T- shirt. They are looking out of the window. In the
street, there is a police car.

2 Write about this picture.

Notes

a man, a woman

having lunch

on the table: some fish,
some bread, a bottle of
wine

the man: a shirt, trousers

the woman: a dress

Paragraph

The picture shows ....
....
....
....
....
....
....

3 Now write about this picture. First write notes, then write a paragraph.

Notes

a man, a woman ....

sitting in a train ....

....

....

....

....

Paragraph

The picture shows ....

....

....

....

....

....

....

13 how much

A Two puzzles

Complete the puzzles.

Puzzle A

1 In the picture, there's a ....

2 There are two ....

3 There are three ....

4 There are four ....

5 There are five ....

C	L	O	C	K

Puzzle B

1 There's a big bottle of .... in the fridge.

2 I always have a cup of .... after lunch.

3 This drink can be red or white.

4 Do you want some .... on your burger?

5 You wash with this.

6 Do you take .... in your tea?

7 $10 million is a lot of ....

8 Elephants drink lots of ....

L	E	M	O	N	A	D	E

Now fill the gaps in these sentences:

In Puzzle A, the answers are all .... nouns. In Puzzle B, the answers are all .... nouns.

B In (and on) the fridge

Imagine this fridge is in your kitchen.
Make sentences like the examples in the box.

We've got lots of	wine. glasses.
We haven't got	much food. many plates.
We haven't got any	coffee. cups.

a We've got lots of ....matches.

b ....cigarettes.

c ....beer.

d ....milk.

e ....eggs.

f ....fruit.

g ....meat.

h ....cheese.

C How much and How many?

These questions are about things in the Classroom Book.
Complete them with *How much* or *How many* + noun.

1 ...How may hotels................................. are there in Ouro Preto?   *See Unit 5*

   About four or five.

2 .... are there in the Empire State Building?   *See Unit 5*

   102.

3 .... do Pizza Hut restaurants use every year?   *See Unit 8*

   160 million kilos.

4 When you give blood, ... do you give?   *See Unit 13*

   About half a litre.

5 .... eat at Burger King restaurants every day?   *See Unit 8*

   More than 13 million.

6 .... are there in the Sultan of Brunei's Palace?   *See Unit 6*

   Nearly 1,800.

7 .... does an average person eat in a lifetime?   *See Unit 13*

   About 30 tonnes.

Listening: *I want ...*

Try to fill the gaps in these
conversations. Use words
from the box.

soap	post a letter
radio	wash my hands
stamps	listen to the news

1 A Excuse me. Have you got a .... here? I want to

   ....

   B Yes, there's one in the kitchen, in the corner by the window.

   B Thanks.

2 A I want to .... Have you got any

   .... ?

   B Sorry, I don't think I've got any. I'll just have a look. No. sorry.

   B Oh.

3 A Food's ready!

   B OK, I just want to .... Have you

   got any .... ?

   A Yes, there's some on the shelf.

   B Oh yes, here it is.

   Now listen and check.

Words

Write these words in your language.

bow	....
envelope	....
key	....
shampoo	....
matches	....
light a fire	....
blood	....
jam	....
fuel	....
elephant	....

Other words

....	....
....	....
....	....
....	....

14 Around the year

A Climate and seasons

What can you remember about these four places? Fill the gaps with words from the box. Use each word *once*.

wet	hot	warm	spring	summer
dry	cold	cool	autumn	winter

1 *Alice Springs*

From October to March, it is very ...., often 40^0 or more. From May to August it is clear and .... by day, but cool at night.

2 *Jakarta*

November to April is the .... season, and in January there is a lot of rain. From July to September it is ...., but the air is always humid.

3 *Istanbul*

In the winter it is .... It open rains in the .... and winter, and it sometimes snows.

4 *Moscow*

Moscow has hot and mainly dry weather in the ...., with temperatures of 25^0 - 30^0 . In the .... it is very .... , and temperatures can be below -20^0. .... comes late in Moscow, usually in April or May.

Check your answers on page 59 of the Classroom Book.

B Months

1 Write the full forms of the months in the table.

2 Complete these sentences.

a .... is the eighth month of the year.

b .... has 28 days. Sometimes it has 29 days.

c New Year's Eve is in ....

d New Year's Day is in ....

e .... is the eleventh month of the year.

f My birthday is in ....

g In my country, the school year begins in .... and finishes in ....

h My favourite month is .... , because ....
....

Jan	
Feb	
Mar	
Apr	
May	May
Jun	
Jul	
Aug	
Sept	September
Oct	
Nov	
Dec	

C Weather

1 Match the sentences with the pictures.

| It's sunny. |
| It's cloudy. |
| It's raining. |
| It's snowing. |
| It's windy. |
| It's humid. |
| ~~It's hot.~~ |
| It's cold. |

1 ....It's hot. ....

2 ....

3 ....

4 ....

5 ....

6 ....

7 ....

8 ....

2 What's the weather like now? Write one or two sentences.

....

....

....

Listening : *Good times, bad times*

Someone from Britain talks about the months he likes, and the months he doesn't like.

Before you listen, read these questions.

1 Why doesn't he like January or February? ....

....

2 What is March like in Britain? ....

3 Why does he like April? ....

4 When is the man's birthday? ....

5 Why does he do in August? ....

6 What happens in September? ....

....

7 Why does he like October? ....

....

8 What is November like? ....

9 What does he do in December? ....

....

 Now listen and answer the questions.

Words

Write these words in your language.

all year round	....
at night	....
temperature	....
air	....
from ... to ...	....
late	....
Christmas	....
holiday	....

Other words

....	....
....	....
....	....
....	....
....	....

Check your progress

1 Look at the table. What can Sue and Jim do? What can't they do?

a They ....

b They ....

c Sue .... the piano.

d Jim .... the piano.

	Sue	Jim
swim	✓	✓
ski	✗	✗
piano	✓	✗

2 Rewrite these sentences using *have* got.

a My brother has long hair.

....

b My parents have a new car.

....

c I don't have much money.

....

d Julia doesn't have a job.

....

3 Write these numbers.

365 ....

1,500 ....

500,000 ....

1,000,000 ....

4

A 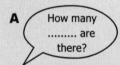 How many .... are there?

B  There isn't much ....

C  We've only got one ....

Which sentences can these words go in? Write A, B or C.

.... food .... meat .... eggs

.... apple .... potatoes .... bottle of lemonade

5 Write the missing words.

a hot - cold wet - .... warm - ....

b .... - summer - autumn - ....

c March - .... - May - .... - July

d It's .... It's ....

Phrasebook

Write these conversations in your language.

Would you like a drink?

No, thanks.

....

....

Would you like an ice-cream?

Yes, please.

....

....

Would you like a lift?

No, thanks.

....

....

Writing: *Birthdays*

1 Look at the sentences . Then read the paragraphs.

Sentences

Birthday: July.

I get up late.

I invite a few friends to my flat.

We have coffee and cakes together.

Paragraph

My birthday is in July. In the morning. I get up late. In the afternoon, I usually invite a few friends to my flat. We have coffee and cake together.

Sentences

Birthday: October.

I get birthday presents from my family.

I got out with a few friends for a drink.

We go to the cinema together.

Paragraph

My birthday is in October. In the morning. I get birthday presents from my family. Then in the evening, I usually go out with a few friends for a drink, or sometimes we go to the cinema together.

in the morning	usually	and
in the afternoon	sometimes	or
in the evening		then

2 Make these sentences into a paragraph. Use words from the box.

Sentences

Birthday: February.

My parents give me presents.

I have a birthday party.

All my friends come.

We play games.

We have a birthday cake.

We eat ice-cream.

Paragraph

My birthday ....
....
....
....
....
....
....

3 Write about your birthday. When is it? What do you do?

....
....
....
....

15 In the past 1

A Verbs in the past

Choose verbs from boxes *A*, *B* and *C* to fill the gaps.

A
was
were

B
asked
looked
opened
phoned
played
wanted

C
gave
had
put
said
saw
took
went

1 Yesterday, it (A) ....was........ my birthday.
and my brother(C) .... me a
birthday present. I (B) .... it.
It (A) .... a cigarette lighter.
'Do you like it?' he (B) .... me.
'Yes. It's lovely', I(C) ....
'But I don't smoke!'
'I'll have it then!' he (C) .... And he (C) .... the lighter out of
my hand. (C) .... it in his pocket and (C) .... out of the room.

2 Yesterday morning. I (A) .... at home alone. My parents (A) ....
out, and I (B) .... to see my friends Bill and Joe. I (B) .... them,
buy they (A) .... out. Then I (B) .... out of the window and
(C) .... them in the street. They (C) .... a ball with them, so we
(C) .... to the park and (B) .... football.

B Say when

Write true sentences about yourself or other people. Use a past time expression in each sentence.

I went to the cinema on Sunday.

I saw "Terminator 2" at the weekend.

My parents went to Canada in 1998.

1 (went) ....
   ....

2 (read) ....
   ....

3 (played)..
   ....

4 (bought) ....
   ....

5 (saw) ....
   ....

Past time expressions		
ON	It happened on Tuesday.	
AT	I saw her at	8 o'clock.
		the weekend.
		the morning.
IN	We went in	September.
		the winter.
		1975.
No preposition with yesterday:		
	It happened	
	I saw her	yesterday.
	We went	

C Past descriptions

Look at these descriptions. Fill the gaps with *was*, *were* and *had*.

1 There .... two people at the bus stop, a man and a woman. They .... about 50 years old. The woman .... quite short and .... no hair at all. They .... a large dog with them. The dog .... long grey hair too.

2 It .... a very good hotel. We .... a lovely room. It .... a double bed, a sofa, a desk and a TV, and it also .... a large balcony. On the balcony there .... three or four chairs, and several plants. There .... a swimming pool in the hotel garden, and there .... also two very good restaurants. We .... a lovely time there!

Listening : *The next morning*

You will hear the end of the story in Unit 15.1 (*Bedtime story*). Listen and mark the sentences T (= true) or F (= false).

1 ☐ My mother was in the living room.

2 ☐ She was with a policeman.

3 ☐ The policeman asked me questions about the man.

4 ☐ I said the man was tall and had dark hair.

5 ☐ The policeman showed me a photo of the man.

6 ☐ The policeman give me some money.

7 ☐ The policeman smiled and said 'Thank you'.

8 ☐ We never saw the man again.

9 ☐ We never saw the policeman again.

10 ☐ We never saw our knives, forks and spoons again.

Words

Write these words in your language.

smile (v.)	....
want	....
late	....
light (n.)	....
game	....
thing	....
wallet	....
purse	....
silver	....
quiet	....
garden	....

Other words

....	....
....	....
....	....
....	....
....	....
....	....
....	....

16 Around the world

A Places

Write the missing words.

1

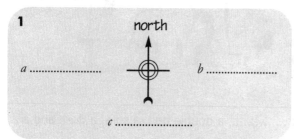

a ....

north

b ....

c ....

2

Where are A, B, C and D ?

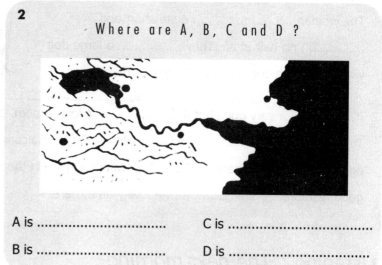

A is ....

B is ....

C is ....

D is ....

3

What's the missing word?

Penang is a tourist ⬚ .... in Malaysia.

St Moritz is a ski .... in Switzerland.

4

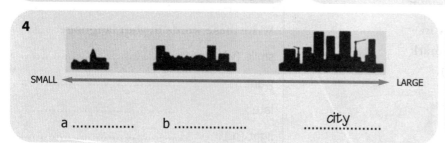

SMALL ⟵——————————————⟶ LARGE

a .... b .... *city* ....

5

Cuba, Tahiti, Borneo, Madagascar and **Corfu** are

all.......................................

B Languages

All the answers are in the wordsquare. Can you find them?

1 *Bonjour, merci* and *s'il vous plaît* – what's the language?

2 The language of Tchaikovsky and Lenin.

3 People in Rio de Janeiro and Lisbon speak this language.

4 *Buenos días, gracias* and *por favor* – what's the language?

5 The language of Confucius and Mao Zedong.

6 People in Warsaw and Krakow speak this language.

7 *Guten Tag, danke, bitte* – what's the language?

8 The language of Pavarotti and Leonardo da Vinci.

9 People in Ankara and Istanbul speak this language.

10 ελληνκά – what's the language?

11 The language of Egypt, Syria and Iraq.

12 People in Tokyo and Osaka speak this language.

There's one more language in the wordsquare. What is it?

```
S P A N I S H Y J
P O L I S H T W A
A R A B I C C I P
E T F T A S H T A
N U R U S S I A N
G G E R M A N L E
L U N K ? E I S
I E C I ? S A E
S S H S ? E N H
H E O H G R E E K
```

C My country

Write a few sentences about your country. Use the questions to help you

> Is it in Europe? Asia? South America?

> Is it a big country? a small country?

> Is it a rich country? a poor country?

> What's the capital city?

....

....

....

....

....

....

....

....

> What language do people speak?

> What about the climate? Is it hot? cold? wet? dry?

Listening: *Other languages*

Two people talk about words they know in other languages. Listen and mark the sentences *T* (= true) or *F* (= false).

Γεία σου

Buongiorno.

1 ☐ The woman can speak French and Spanish.

2 ☐ She learned French at school.

3 ☐ She lives in Greece.

4 ☐ She knows a lot of Greek.

5 ☐ She can say Yes in Arabic.

6 ☐ The woman and the man both know a few words of Italian.

7 ☐ The man speaks Japanese quite well.

8 ☐ The man knows a few words of Russian.

Write these words in your language.

port	....
tourist	....
ferry	....
centre	....
holiday	....
visit	....
route	....
best	....
language	....
love (v.)	....

Other words

....	....
....	....
....	....
....	....
....	....
....	....
....	....

H Study pages

Check your progress

1 Write these dates in the words.

14th Feb ....

22 Aug ....

28 Oct ....

31st Dec ....

2 Put the mixed up words in the right order.

a a them letter wrote I

.... yesterday.

b me bring water of can a glass you

.... please?

c gave money I her some

.... for her birthday.

3 Fill the gaps with *in* or *on*.

When I was a child, I lived (a)........... a village (b)..............
the south coast. Now I live (c)........... a town (d)..............
the north-east. It's a beautiful place: it's high up (e).............
the mountains, and it's (f).............. a lake.

4 Read the text, and write about yesterday.

Every day, Paul and Lola have breakfast. Then they take the
dog to the park. Paul buy a newspaper and reads it. Lola
walks through the park and plays with the dog. Then they
go home and watch TV.

Yesterday, Paul and Lola ....

....

....

....

....

....

5 Write the languages.

a France ....   *d* Poland ....

b China ....   *e* Japan ....

c Russia...........................   *f* Greece...........................

Phrasebook

Write these conversations in your language.

....

....

....

....

....

....

....

....

....

Writing: *and, so, because*

1 Look at these sentences.

I opened the door.

I went into the garden. → I opened the door and went into the garden.

I wanted a drink.

I went to a café. → I wanted a drink, so I went to a café.

I took an umbrella.

It was very wet. → I took an umbrella *because* it was very wet.

2 Fill the gaps with *and, so* or *because*. Then check your answers in the Classroom Book.

15.1 Bedtime story

It was very late at night, ... my parents were asleep. I was awake .... I wanted to go to the toilet. I went to the toilet, ... I saw a light under the living room door .... I opened the door .... went in, ... I saw a man in the living room.

16.4 International travel

She called room service .... ordered a chicken sandwich and a beer. Then she felt tired, ... she went back into the room .... went to sleep.

3 Join these sentences. Use *and, so* or *because*.

a I went to bed early last night.   ....

   I was tired.   ....

b It was cold.   ....

   I went to a clothes shop.   ....

   I bought a jumper.   ....

c My mother was a teacher at my school ....

   We went there together every morning. ....

d When I was young, we listened to the radio. ....

   We didn't have a TV.   ....

A It's all wrong!

These sentences are all wrong.
Look at the pictures and
correct them.

1

2

3

On Saturday morning, Paul and Julia went to the beach.

They bought a new fridge.

They had chicken for lunch.

4

5

6

7

In the afternoon, they played cards ...

... and then they went to a party.

They got home at ten o'clock ...

... and watched a football match on TV.

1 They didn't go to the beach. They went to the town centre. . . . .

2 They didn't . . . .

3 . . . .

4 . . . .

5 . . . .

6 . . . .

7 . . . .

B Yes/no questions

When you went to New York last year...

... the people were friendly.

... the weather was hot.

... the restaurants were good.

... you went to the theatre.

... you visited the Empire State Building.

... you walked in Central Park.

... you had a good time.

to be	
The film <u>was</u> good.	→ <u>Was</u> the film good?
They <u>were</u> at home.	→ <u>Were</u> they at home?

Other verbs

She <u>watched</u> TV.	→ <u>Did</u> she <u>watch</u> TV?
He <u>saw</u> the film.	→ <u>Did</u> he <u>see</u> the film?

Last month, some friends went to New York for a holiday. Ask them about their holiday.

1 Were the people friendy? . . . .

2 . . . .

3 . . . .

4 Did you . . . .

5 . . . .

6 . . . .

7 . . . .

C Wh- questions

A police officer answers some questions. Read his notes, then write the missing questions.

1 - *What time did he arrive at the café?* ....

  - At 9.15.

2 - ....

  - In the corner, by the window.

3 - ....

  - At 9.25.

4 - ....

  - An envelope.

5 - ....

  - Some money.

6 - ....

  - About £100.

7 - ....

  - At 9.37.

> He arrived at the café at 9.15. He sat in the corner, by the window. She came in at 9.25, and sat next to him. He gave her an envelope, and she gave him some money – about 100. She left at 9.37.

Listening: *Can you remember?*

🖭 **A man answers the questions in Unit 17.3 (*Memory text*). Listen and fill the gaps.**

1 *The last time I bought some clothes*

  I bought .... at the Jean Machine.

  They cost ....

2 *Last Sunday*

  The weather was ....
  .... I had ....
  ....
  for breakfast. I got up at ....

3 *The last time I went to a party*

  I wrote ....
  I arrived at .... and left at ....

Words

Write these words in your language.

paint (v.)	....
start (v.)	....
arrive	....
die	....
war	....
play (n.)	....
concert	....
programme	....
interesting	....
boring	....
fireworks	....

Other words

....

....

....

How to get there

A Prepositions

Choose prepositions to fill the gaps.

across	along	down	into	out of	over	past	through	up

1 He's going .... the house. 2 He's coming .... the house. 3 She's going .... the house.

4 She's going .... the steps. 5 She's going .... the steps. 6 He's climbing .... the wall.

7 She's climbing .... the window. 8 She's going .... the road. 9 He's going .... the bridge.

B Moving around

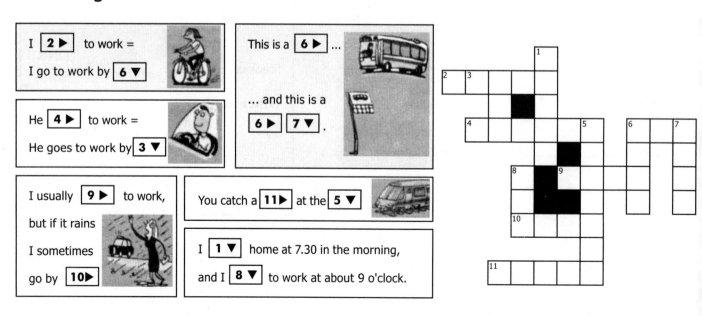

I [2 ▶] to work =
I go to work by [6 ▼]

He [4 ▶] to work =
He goes to work by [3 ▼]

I usually [9 ▶] to work,
but if it rains
I sometimes
go by [10▶]

This is a [6 ▶] ...
... and this is a
[6 ▶] [7 ▼].

You catch a [11▶] at the [5 ▼]

I [1 ▼] home at 7.30 in the morning,
and I [8 ▼] to work at about 9 o'clock.

C Giving directions

1 Make five sentences from the table, giving directions to there cinema.

Go straight	at the chemist.
There's a chemist	on the right.
Turn right	along this road.
Go past	on the corner.
The cinema's	the church.

....

....

....

....

....

2 Write your own directions from   to the swimming pool.

....

....

....

Listening: *Bags of gold*

🖭 Listen to the directions and find the bags of gold. Which bags are they?

1 = ...   2 = ...   3 = ...   4 = ...

Words

Write these words in your language.

ladder	....
hut	....
path	....
rope	....
tunnel	....
outside	....
at the end	....
Carry straight on	....

Other words

....

....

....

....

....

....

Study pages

Check your progress

1 Write two short answers, one positive and one negative.

a   Did you go to the shops?   Yes,....................................   No,....................................

b   Were your parents at home?   ....

           ....

c   Is there any milk in the fridge?   ....

           ....

2 Complete the sentences.

a Our car isn't very fast.   = It's quite.............................

b Her hair's quite short.   = It isn't very.............................

c Rice isn't very expensive. = ...

d My sister's quite young.   = ...

3 Write these years in words.

1760 ....

1999 ....

2001 ....

4 Look at these answers. What are the questions?

a   Did you ....

     Yes (I went to John's birthday party).

b   Where ....

     (It was) at his parents' flat.

c   ....

     (I wore) my new green dress.

d   ....

Yes (I enjoyed it).

e   ....

(I got home) at two o'clock in the morning.

5 Fill the gaps with prepositions.

The man goes.......................... the house, ... the road, ... the steps, ... the bridge, ... the steps and .... the shop.

Phrasebook

Write these conversations in your language.

Let's cycle to the station.

That's a good idea.

....

....

Shall we take a taxi?

No. Let's walk.

....

....

Shall we go?

No, not yet.

....

....

Writing: *Then ...*

1 Look at the sentences and the paragraph.

Sentences

It was Monday morning.

Andreas got up early.
He had a shower.
He put on a grey suit.

He had breakfast.
He listened to the news on the radio.

Paragraph

It was Monday morning. Andreas got up early, had a shower and put on a grey suit. *Then* he had breakfast *and* listened to the news on the radio.

2 Continue the story. Join the sentences together. Use commas (,), *and* and *then*.

Sentences

At 7 o'clock he left home.
He walked to the station.
He took a train to London.

He took a bus to his office building.
He went up to the 10th floor.

He went into his office.
He sat at his desk.
He started work.

Paragraph

....
....
....
....
....
....
....
....

3 What did you do last Monday morning? Write sentences. Then join them together into a paragraph.

Sentences

....
....
....
....
....
....
....
....
....
....

Paragraph

....
....
....
....
....
....
....
....
....

19 You mustn't do that!

A Must and mustn't

What are these people saying? Complete the sentences with *You must* or *You mustn't*.

1

....You must............... have a shower.

.... wash your hair.

.... wear those shoes in the house.

2

.... drink lots of water.

.... ho to school.

.... stay in bed.

3

.... stay up late.

.... clean your teeth.

.... be good!

B Can and can't

Imagine you're staying in a friend's flat. What can you do? What can't you do?

1 ....You can watch a film... (There's a TV in the living room.)

2 ....You can't have a hot shower.................................... (There isn't any hot water.)

3 .... (There isn't any shampoo.)

4 .... (There's a CD player.)

5 .... (There's a pen and paper in the desk.)

6 .... (There isn't a computer.)

7 .... (There's lots of food in the fridge.)

8 .... (There isn't a pack of cards.)

C I have to go home

Make sentences with *have to, has to, don't have to* and *doesn't have to.*

Positive	Negative
I have to go.	We don't have to go.
She has to go.	He doesn't have to go.

1 I can't stay here. ......I have to go home.................. (go home)

2 She can stay in bed. ...She doesn't have to get up......... (get up)

3 You can wear jeans. .... (wear a suit)

4 We can go to a restaurant. .... (cook a meal)

5 He can't go out. ....
.... (do his homework)

6 You can't use the lift. ....
.... (go down the stairs)

7 They can stay with us. ....
.... (stay in a hotel)

8 She can go by taxi. .... (walk)

Listening: *House rules*

A man is staying in this room. The landlady tells him what he can and can't do.

 Listen and look at the picture. Find things that are wrong and put a circle round them.

Words

Write these words in your language.

gun ....

stop (v) ....

animals ....

take a photo ....

polite ....

careful ....

hard ....

dangerous ....

cleaner ....

fishing boat ....

Other words

....

....

....

....

....

20 The body

A Parts of the body

Complete the crossword. All the answers are parts of the body.

1 ▶ You wear a tie round your . . . . .

2 ▼ You see with your . . . . .

3 ▼ You have to open your . . . . when you eat or speak.

4 ▶ Your . . . . is in the centre of your face.

5 ▶ You wear a hat on your . . . . .

6 ▼ You have two . . . . - one on each side of your body.

7 ▼ Your . . . . are on the ends of your 6.

8 ▶ People wear rings on their . . . . .

8 ▼ You wear shoes on your . . . . .

9 ▼ You hear with your . . . . .

10 ▶ Dogs, cats and elephants have four . . . . .People have two.

B Using the body

What are the people doing? Use verbs from the box.

catch	climb	jump	kick	~~ride~~	~~run~~	stand	swim	throw	walk

1 ....

2 ....

3 ....

4 ....

5 ....

6 ....

7 ....

8 ....

9 ....

10 ....

C Where did he go?

1 Write the past forms of the verbs in the box.

2 Can you remember the story in Exercise 20.3 in the Classroom Book? Complete the sentences. Use these key expressions to help you.

across the island	up the rock	across the sea
to a rock	out of the house	off the bridge
to an island	into the river	to an airport

climb	....
drive	....
fly	....
jump	....
ride	....
run	..*ran*..........
swim	....

1 (run) ....The man ran..

2 (drive) ....He..

3 (fly) ....

4 (ride) ....

5 (jump) ....

6 (swim) ....

7 (climb) ....

Listening: *Exercises*

Do you understand these phrases? If not, look in a dictionary.

stand up	sit down	lie down
cross (your legs)	raise (your arm)	straight

Listen to these exercises. Write numbers by the pictures.

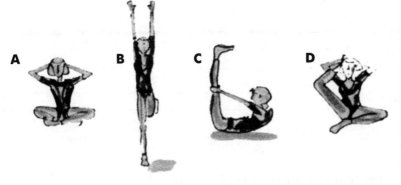

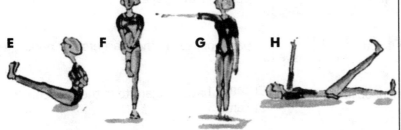

Words

Write these words in your language.

careful ....

friendly ....

human ....

stream ....

in the middle ....

at the top ....

metre ....

kilometre ....

chocolate bar ....

Other words ....

....

....

....

....

....

....

....

Study pages

Check your progress

1 Can you remember the story in the Classroom Book? Make adverbs and fill the gaps.

ellw	lloswy	ciklquy
agilnry	acefllruy	~~eddlnsuy~~	eilqtuy

I woke *(a)* ......suddenly............... at 6 o'clock. Marie was by my bed. 'Get dressed *(b)* .... , 'she said, 'or we'll be late'. .....We closed the front door *(c)* .... and got in the car. Marie drove *(d)* .... -fast but *(e)* .... -and we got to the harbour by 7 o'clock .... As we moved *(f)* .... out of the harbour, a black car came round the corner. It was Carlos.' Marie ! Come back!' he shouted *(g)* .... But he was too late.

2 Fill the gaps with *to* , *at* and *about*.

a Don't listen .... him! He always talks .... football.

b I went .... London last weekend, and stayed .... a friend's flat.

c OK. Look .... the picture on page 20, and listen .... the recording.

3 Write one word in each gap.

a head, face, eyes, ..., ..., ...,

b body, neck, arms,................, ...,

c kick a ball, ... a ball, ...a ball

d ride a bike, ... a car, ... a plane, ... a horse

4 Here are some rules for students at a language school. Choose the right verbs.

a You ☐ can / ☐ must buy your own books, but you ☐ can't / ☐ don't have to buy your own tapes

b You ☐ can / ☐ have to drive to the school, but you ☐ mustn't / ☐ don't have to park your car in the teachers' car park.

c You ☐ can't / ☐ don't have to smoke in the school building, but you ☐ can / ☐ can't have a cigarette in the garden.

Phrasebook

Write these conversations in your language.

> Could you buy me a magazine?

> Yes, of course

....
....
....

> Could you bring me some cigarettes?

> No, sorry.

....
....
....

Writing: *Animals*

1 Look at the picture and the notes. Then read the paragraph.

Elephants
very large

grey

live in Africa/India

eat leaves

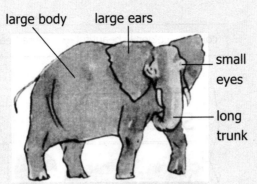

large body   large ears

small eyes

long trunk

Elephants *are grey, and they are* very large animals. *They have* a large body, large ears *and* a long trunk, *but* very small eyes. *They live* in India and Africa *and they* eat leaves.

2 Fill the gaps in this paragraph.

Penguins
usually black and white

can't fly

can swim very well

live by the sea

eat fish

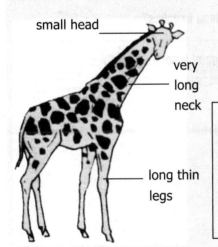

very small wings

short legs   large feet

Penguins .... usually black and white. .... short legs .... large feet. .... very small wings .... can't fly, ... can swim very well, ... live by the sea .... eat fish.

3 Choose one of these animals. Make the notes into a paragraph.

small head

very long neck

long thin legs

Giraffes
very tall

brown and white

eat leaves

can run fast

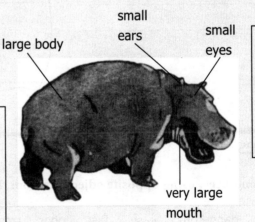

large body   small ears   small eyes

very large mouth

Hippos
large animals

grey

live in rivers

dangerous

Rabbits
quite small

brown

can run very fast

eat grass

very long ears

large eyes

small white tail

....

....

....

....

....

....

21 Good, better, best

A Tourist resorts

Look at the information and
compare the two tourist resorts.

1 Seatown is hotter in summer.

2 ....

   ....

   ....

3 ....

   ....

4 ....

   ....

5 Merville has friendlier people
   than Seatown.

6 ....

   ....

7 ....

   ....

8 ....

   ....

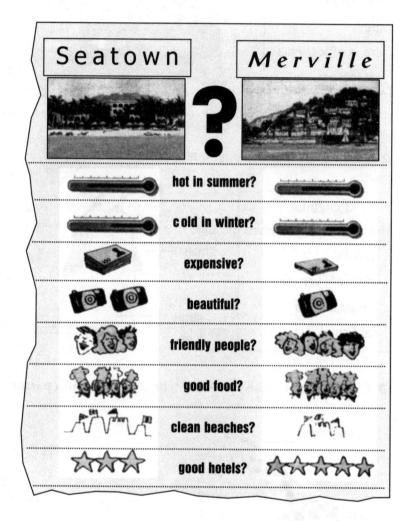

Seatown   **?**   **Merville**

hot in summer?
cold in winter?
expensive?
beautiful?
friendly people?
good food?
clean beaches?
good hotels?

B Opposites

Change these sentences, using opposite adjectives from the box.

| cheap | cool | dangerous | easy | fast | poor | small | weak |

1 Los Angeles is bigger than San Francissco. San Francissco is smaller than Los Angeles.

2 Beef is more expensive than chicken. ....

3 Cars are safer than motorbikes. ....

4 Russian is more difficult than English. ....

5 George is stronger than Fred. ....

6 Buses are slower than trains. ....

7 August is warmer than October. ....

8 Bill Gates is richer than me. I'm ....

C Who's the tallest?

Can you do these puzzles?

tall → the tallest	expensive → the more expensive

Puzzle 1: tall and short

Alice is taller than Ben, but she's shorter than Carlos.
Danka is taller than Carlos.

1 ..Danka is the tallest................................(tall)

2 ....(short)

Puzzle 2: big and small

I have four boxes: A, B, C and D.
There are three boxes inside Box
B, two boxes inside Box A, and
one box inside Box C.

3 .... (big)

4 ....(small)

Puzzle 3: old and young

Hannah is older than Eva, but younger than Fred.
George is 16 years old, and Eva is 21.

5 .... (old)

6 ....(young)

Puzzle 4: fast, slow, cheap, and expensive

There are three cars. The BMW is more expensive
than the Honda, but it's slower. The Ford's cheaper
than the Honda, and it's faster, too.

7..(fast)

8...(slow)

9..(cheap)

10...(expensive)

Listening: *Buying things*

🔲 **Listen to the three conversation, and fill the gaps.**

Conversation 1

A man wants to buy .... He chooses

the one for £45 because it's   .... than

the other one.

Conversation 2

A woman wants to buy .... for

.............................She chooses the ones for £15

because they're .... than the other ones.

Conversation 3

A man wants to buy ....He chooses

the one for £45 because it's   ....

than the other one.

Words

Write these words in your language.

better ....

best ....

agree ....

disagree ....

difficult ....

actor ....

use(v.) ....

probably ....

different ....

Other words

....

....

....

....

....

22 Free time

A Last week

Look at these examples.

> Activity 5 Last Tuesday I went to the cinema with a friend. We saw the new James Bond film.

> Activity 9 Last weekend, we went for a drive in the mountains, and had lunch in a restaurant.

> Activity 4 Last Saturday I went shopping in the town centre. I bought a jacket and some cassettes.

The *Top* **10** Activities

1 visit friends or relatives
2 go out for a drink or a meal
3 go for a walk or a bike ride
4 go shopping for fun
5 go to a cinema, concert or sports event
6 do an outdoor sport
7 do an indoor sport
8 follow an interest or hobby
9 go for a drive or a picnic
10 go swimming

Which of the 10 activities did you do last week? Write about them.

Activity ....Last...

....

Activity ....

....

Activity ....

....

B Likes and dislikes

What do these people like doing?
What don't they like doing?
Make sentences from the table.

He	likes	getting up early. washing the dishes.
	enjoys	playing tennis. having a bath.
She	doesn't like	staying up late. eating.
	doesn't enjoy	watching tennis. washing his hair.

1 ..She like...
   ..but she doesn't like..

2 ....
   ....

3 ....
   ....

4 ....
   ....

C Sports

The ten mixed-up words are all sports.
Which do you go, and which do you *play*?

ABELLLOVY	BCGIILMN
GIIKNS	GIIMMNSW ✓
FGLO	EINNST	ABFLLOOT
GINNNUR	DFGIINNRSUW
AABBEKLLST

| go | Swimming ....
 ....
 ....
 ....
 .... | play | ....
 ....
 ....
 ....
 .... |

Listening : *At the weekend*

Four people say what they like doing at the weekend.
Listen and write numbers (1, 2, 3, 4) in the boxes.

He/She likes ...

a | 1, 3, 4 | ... getting up late.

b [ ] ... getting up early.

c [ ] ... doing sport.

d [ ] ... doing housework.

e [ ] ... doing nothing.

f [ ] ... going out.

g [ ] ... staying at home.

h [ ] ... spending time with friends.

i [ ] ... having a big breakfast.

Words

Write these words in your language.

relatives ....

sports event ....

hobby ....

bike ride ....

spend money ....

lose weight ....

physical
exercise ....

indoors ....

out of doors ....

local ....

Other words

....

....

....

Check your progress

1 Complete these conversations.

a - Would .... play tennis this evening?

  - No, thanks. But I'd .... play cards.

b - Do .... come to a party tonight?

  - Sorry, I can't. .... do my homework.

2 Fill the gaps with *to*, *in*, for *or* - (=nothing).

a In the morning, I always go .... a run before I

  go .... work.

b He goes .... out every evening, and he goes

  .... bed at 2 o'clock in the morning.

c - Did you go .... swimming yesterday?

  - No, we went .... a drive.

d Does anyone need to go .... the toilet?

3 Compare the cars.

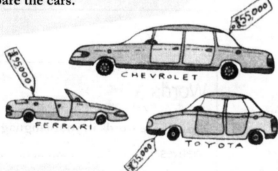

a Toyota/big/Ferrari

  ....

b Ferrari/expensive/Chevrolet

  ....

c ....(small)

d ....(big)

e ....(expensive)

4 Can you remember the story? Write one word in each gap.

United were one of the best football .... in

the country, but their .... wasn't very big.

They built a new .... That season, United

.... a lot of matches in other football

grounds. But they .... all the matches they

played at home.

Phrasebook

Write these replies in your language.

....

....

....

....

....

....

Writing : *and, but, also*

1 Look at these examples.

✓	walking
✓	swimming
✓	playing football

I like walking *and* swimming, and *I also* enjoy playing football.

✓	cooking
(✓)	cleaning
✗	washing dishes

I enjoy cooking *and* I quite like cleaning, *but* I don't like washing dishes.

✓	bread
✓	rice
✓	pasta
✓	beans
✓	onions
✗	potatoes

I like bread, rice *and* pasta. I *also* like beans and onions. *But* I don't like potatoes very much

> Note
> also comes before the main verb:
> 1 2   3
> I also enjoy playing football.

2 Write paragraphs about these things.

✓	driving
✓	cycling
✓	going by train
✓	going by bus
✗	flying

....
....
....
....

✓	vanilla ice-cream
✓	strawberry ice-ream
(✓)	chocolate ice-cream
✗	coffee ice-cream

....
....
....

3 Answer two of these questions . Write paragraphs.

What pop singers do you like?

What drinks do you like?

What do you like doing in the evening?

What sports do you like watching?

....
....
....
....
....
....

23 Future plans

A Going to ...

What do you think these people are going to do?
Use two ideas from the box, and add one idea of your own.

have a shower	drink champagne
eat ice-creams	play in the sand
have a cup of coffee	talk to friends

1

He's just arrving home after a hard day's work.

He's going to ....

....

....

2

They're just arriving at the beach.

....

....

....

3

She's just arriving at a birthday party.

....

....

....

B Questions with 'going to'

1 *match United when to going a win are?*

2 *bus going time the arrive is what to?*

3 *to you what party to going are wear the?*

4 *home we to are get how going?*

5 *where to it you are going put?*

What are the questions?

1 *When are United* ....

2 ....

3 ....

4 ....

5 ....

C When is it happening?

Write sentences about some future events. Say when they're happening.

| On Saturday, Manchester United are playing Juventus. |
| I'm going to a party tomorrow evening. |
| On September 7th, the President is going to China. |
| We're watching a video this afternoon. |
| My parents are moving to a new flat next year. |

this (evening)

tomorrow

....

tomorrow (morning)

....

at the weekend

....

next week

....

next (Tuesday)

....

in the (summer)

....

in (October)

on (15th July)

Listening: *At the airport*

You will hear four people at Heathrow Airport, London. Listen and fill the gaps.

1 He's .... in Tokyo for two days, then

   he's .... to Osaka.

2 They're ....to the Canary Islands.

   They're .... for two weeks.

3 He's .... in Rome, and then he's

   .... to the south of Italy.

4 Her uncle .... from Switzerland, and

   she's .... to her flat in London.

Now answer these questions

a What is the man doing in Osaka?

....

b How long is he staying in Japan?

....

c How is the woman getting to her hotel?

....

d Why is the man going to stay at camp-sites?

....

e How long is the woman's uncle staying with her?

....

Words

Write these words in your language.

spend (time)   ....

a few days   ....

plan (v.)   ....

sure   ....

exactly   ....

carefully   ....

housework   ....

late   ....

move (v.)   ....

look after   ....

Other words

....

....

....

....

A Suggestions

Look at these suggestions. How is the other person feeling? Fill the gaps with words from the box.

| cold |
| hot |
| hungry |
| ill |
| thirsty |
| tired |

1 - I feel .... - Shall I phone the doctor?

2 - I'm really .... - Shall I get you a drink?

3 - I feel a bit .... - Why don't you go to bed early tonight?

4 - I'm a bit .... - Why don't you put on your coat?

5 - I'm feel .... - Let's go inside, out of the sun.

6 - I'm .... - Let's go and get a pizza.

Look at the conversations again, and write your own suggestions.

1 ....

2 ....

3 ....

4 ....

5 ....

6 ....

| Shall I...? |

| Why don't you...? |

| Let's... |

B How do they feel?

How do these people feel? Find answers in the mixed-up words.

| DSA |
| PRESSRUDI |
| ✓ DETECIX |
| NYRAG |
| DEFERTHING |
| PHYPA |
| PETSU |

1

.... excited ....

2

....

3

....

4

....

5

....

6

....

7

....

C What do you think?

Which TV programmes do you like? Which don't you like? Why?
Choose three programmes and write one or two sentences about them.

1 ....
   ....
   ....

2 ....
   ....
   ....

3 ....
   ....
   ....

Listening: *Three stories*

Listen to the three stories and fill the gaps.

Story 1

A woman bought .... and drove it into

town to .... Someone threw a

brick .... and ....

.... She felt very ....

....

Story 2

A man was in a plane on the way to London. The weather

was .... , and the plane started to

.... Everyone felt very

.... but after a few minutes

....

Story 3

A girl went to .... with

.... She felt very .... ,

and she .... the night before

They arrived early, so they ....

Words

Write these words in your language.

a bit	....
really	....
have a rest	....
invite	....
laugh	....
cry	....
hold (held)	....
boring	....
interesting	....
funny	....

Other words

....	....
....	....
....	....
....	....
....	....
....	....
....	....
....	....

Final review

Positive and negative (8 points)

Make these sentences negative.

Examples: He's French. ~~He isn't French.~~............

1 They're rich.

....

2 I drive a Mercedes.

....

3 My brother eats meat.

....

4 We're got a dog.

....

5 There's some beer in the fridge.

....

6 Drink that!

....

7 They went by train.

....

8 She has to get up early.

....

Lists (15 points)

Add to these lists.

Examples: red, green, ...blue.... ...orange.... ..brown...

mother, ...father..... ; brother, ...sister....

1 wife, ...; son, ...

2 bathroom, bedroom, ...

3 knife, ... spoon; salt, ...

4 clothes shop, post office, kiosk, bookshop, ...

....

5 jacket, shirt, trousers, dress, hat ....

....

6 January, ... March, ... May

7 .... south, east, ...

8 plane, car, ...

9 head, face, neck, arms, ...

....

10 happy, sad, ...

Verbs (15 points)

Fill the gaps, using the verbs in brackets.

Example: My flat (have) ....has....... a balcony, but the rooms (be) ....are....... vely small.

1 Mimi and Yves are from France. They (live) .... in Paris. Mimi (be) .... a teacher: she (teach) .... maths at the university. Yves (work) .... in a bank.

2 In the picture ,there's a man. He (have) .... dark hair, and he (wear) .... a white suit. He (stand) .... on a high bridge, and he (look) .... down at the water.

3 Yesterday morning. I (get) .... up at 8.30 and (go) .... to the shops. I (buy) .... a newspaper and some cigarettes. Then I (sit) .... in my favourite café, (have) .... a cup of coffee, (read) .... my newspaper and (smoke) .... a cigarette.

Numbers and words (5 points)

Write the _underlined_ parts of the sentences in words.

Example: Our flat is on the _6th_ floor, ...sixth......

1 He lives at _318_ Brighton Road.

....

2 There are about _1.700.000_ people in this city.

....

3 The time is exactly _11.45_.

....

4 My mother's birthday is _22nd Nov._

....

5 Elvis Presley died in _1977_.

....

Questions (20 points)

Here are some answers. What are the questions?

Example: Q ...What's her name?...

Q A *(Her name's)* Paula.

1 Q ....

A *(I'm from)* Berlin.

2 Q ....

A Yes, these is (*a TV in my bedroom*).

3 Q ....

A (*There are*) Fifteen (*students in the class*).

4 Q ....

A (*She starts work*) At 8.30.

5 Q ....

A (*They're staying*) At the Metropolitan Hotel.

6 Q ....

A (*There's*) About half a kilo (*of rice*).

7 Q ....

A (*He arrived*) This morning.

8 Q ....

A Yes, I was (*at home yesterday*).

9 Q ....

A Yes, she can (*speak French*).

10 Q ....

A (*I'm going to wear*) Jeans and a T-shirt.

Conversations (10 points)

Write *one* word in each gap.

Examples: - How are you?

- I'm ......fine......, thanks.

1 - .... I have some juice, please?

- Yes, of course. .... you are.

2 - Hello. 245670.

- Hello. Is Mr Jones ...., please ?

- Sorry. He's out at the moment.

- OK. Never ....

3 - .... up! We're late!

- OK. Wait just a .... !

4 - .... you like something to eat?

- No, ... I'm not hungry.

5 - What .... 'voz' mean?

- Sorry. I have no ....

Prepositions (10 points)

Write prepositions in the gaps.

Example: Go straight.....along..... this street.

1 In the picture:

- the bag's

....

the desk.

- the lamp's

....

the desk.

- the umbrella's .... the bag.

- the shoes are .... the desk.

- the boxes are .... the desk and the wall.

2 I spoke to him .... Sunday. He phoned

.... 4 o'clock .... the afternoon.

3 London is .... the south of England.

It's .... the River Thames.

Nouns, adjectives and verbs (17 points)

1 Write languages.

In Argentina, people speak ....

People in Istanbul and Ankara ...speak................. .

In Moscow, people speak ....

People in Egypt and Syria speak ....

2 Write opposites.

high ....   weak ....

easy ....   fast ....

3 Complete the sentences.

Everest is the .... mountain in the world.

The Nile is the .... river in the world.

I'm taller than you. You're .... than me.

I'm smaller than him. He's .... than me.

4 Write verbs.

The man flew to an island. Then he ....

a horse across the island, ... off a

bridge into a river, ... to a high

rock, ... up the rock and got

a chocolate bar. He ....

the chocolate bar to his wife.

Tapescripts

Unit 1 Photos

1 This is my friend Julia. She's a student in London.
2 This is my flat in London. It's a big flat – it's quite old.
3 This is John. He's a teacher and he's from the USA.
4 This is my car. It's new, but it's very small.
5 These are my friends Bill and Graham. They're from Australia.

Unit 2 Parents and children

1 We have two children, a boy and a girl. The boy's six years old and the girl's three.
2 I have two children, a girl and a boy. The girl's eleven and the boy's nine.
3 We have three children: two boys – they're both at school – and a baby girl.
4 Well, we have two children – they're both girls. One is 20 – she's married, and she has a baby of six months. And the other girl is still at school – she's 16.

Unit 3 Spell the words

Well, in the picture you can see a ring, that's number 1, a ring – r-i-n-g. And the ring has a diamond, that's number 2, a diamond – d-i-a-m-o-n-d. And then numbers 3 and 4 are an orange: o-r-a-n-g-e, and an apple: a-p-p-l-e. And number 5 is a lamp: l-a-m-p, and number 6 is a plant: p-l-a-n-t. And then there's a picture of a mountain, that's number 7: m-o-u-n-t-a-i-n. In fact, it's Mount Fuji, in Japan.

Unit 4 Birthday presents

1 Well, I got a watch from my mother and father, and I got a CD from my brother.
2 I got a new pen from my parents, and dark blue jumper.
3 I got a football and a football jumper.
4 I got a camera and a book.
5 I got a computer.
6 I got some books, and a very nice. bag for school – it's a sort of green and grey colour.
7 I got a new dress – it's yellow and white – and some white shoes.

Unit 5 Language school

A OK, well, this is the school. It's on two floors – there are five class-rooms altogether, and there's a café for the students.
B Oh, right. How many students are there?
A At the moment about 200. it's quite a small school.
B Right. And do you have a library?
A Yes, there's a small library for the students – we have about 100 books. And we have three comput-ers, too – they're in the library.
B Do you have videos?
A Yes, there's a video in every classroom.
B Right, and how many teachers are there?
A We have six teachers. And the classes are quite small – about 10 to 15 students in each class, never more than 15
B Hmm, that sounds good. What's this in here, then ...?

Unit 6 Who are you ?

A Right- can I have your first name, please?
B Susan.
A And your last name?
B Kennedy.
A Can you spell that?
B Yes, it's K-E-double N_E_D_Y.
A And what's your address?
B It's 23 Abbot Road.
A That's A ...
B A-double B-O-T Road ... London.
A London. Ok ...post code?
B Yes, it's SW1A2JW
A And what's your phone number, please?
B 0181 622 6460.
A OK. Thank you very much.

Unit 7 I like ...

A What food do you like, Marianne?
B I like pizza, I like spaghetti ... I like Italian ice-ream.
A What about drinks?
B Well, I don't drink alcohol – never. And I don't like tea or coffee. I usually drink just water, or maybe orange juice.
A What about music?
B Yes. I like music a lot. I often listen to music in the evening, at home. And I play the piano.
A What about clothes? What are your favourite colours?
B Well, I don't like dark colours. I usually wear light colours – light green, light grey, white, yellow maybe.
A And what about languages ? What languages do you speak?
B Well, I'm from English, so of course I speak English. And I also speak French – a bit. And that's all, really.

Unit 8 In a restaurant

Conversation 1
A Are you ready to order, madam?
B Yes, I'd like the chicken, please, and a green salad.
A Anything the drink?
B Yes, A Coca-Cola, please.
A And for you, sir?
C I'd like spaghetti. And I'll have a green salad, too.
A Spaghetti and green salad. Ok
C And to drink ... I'll have a beer, please.
A Beer. Thank you

Conversation 2
A Yes, sir?
B I'd like fish, but not with rice. Can I have it with potatoes?
A I'm sorry, sir, the fish is only with rice.
B Oh. Well, I'll have the chicken then. And I'd like vegetables - what are the vegetables?
A Sorry, sir, no vegetables today. Only salad.
B Hmm. Ring, Ok, I'll have tomato salad, then.
A Anything to drink?
B Yes. Do you have wine?
A No, sir. Only beer.
B Hmm - a glass of water, then, please.

Unit 9 When are they together?

1 Well, actually I work for a radio station. It's a 24-hour station, and I work at night. So I go to work at 8 o'clock in the evening, and I get home at 4 in the morning. Then I go to bed, and I get up at about half past 12 and have lunch. Then in the afternoon I watch TV, usually, or read. And I have dinner at 7 o'clock, and then it's time to go to work again.

2 I work in a supermarket. I get up at 8 o'clock in the morning and have breakfast, and then I go to work. And I get home from work at a quarter to 6, asually, and I have dinner at around seven in the evening. Then I watch TV or read, and I go to bed at about 11 o'clock.

Unit 10 Shopping

1 A I'll have six oranges, please.
   B Six oranges. Anything else?
   A Yes, three kilos of potatoes, please, and half a kilo of green beans. And that's all, thanks.
   B Ok . That's £2.60 altogether.
2 A An evening paper, please.
   B Ok, that's 35, please. Anything else?
   A Yes. Do you have a street map?
   B Yes, we do
   A How much are they?
   B £1.30.
   A Ok, I'll have one please.
   B Ok, that's £1.65 altogether, then
3 A How much are these jumpers?
   B £45.
   A Do you have any other colour?
   B No, sorry. Just yellow and dark blue.
   A Hmm. OK, I'll just have this T-shirt, then.
   B The T-shirt? That's 18, please

Unit 11 On the phone

1 A Hello. Is Ali there, please?
   B Yes, I think so. I think he's in his room, he's watching the football match. Just a minute, I'll get him for you.
   A OK, thanks.
2 A Hello. Can I speak to Susie, please?
   B Sorry, she's out at the moment. She's at the cinema.
   A Oh. OK, never mind.
3 A Is Sam there, please?
   B Yes, Who's that?
   A It's Mike.
   B Oh, hello, Mike. Look, I'm afraid Sam's doing his homework at the moment.
   A Oh. OK, I'll phone again later.
4 A Can I speak to Mrs Lopez, please?
   B Sorry, she isn't here at the moment, it's her lunchbreak. She's having somewhere.
   A OK, never mind. Thank you.

Unit 12 Where are the Browns?

Ok, that's Mr brown. He's wearing a jacket and trousers, no tie, and he's talking to the woman with the long dark hair – she's wearing a black dress. Now Mrs Brown is over there. She's wearing the skirt and a blouse, and she's talking to a tall man with fair hair. And their son, Richard ... yes, there he is , he's over in the corner. He' wearing jean and a T-shirt – he's the one with very short hair.

Unit 13 I want ...

1 A Excuse me. Have you got a radio here? I want to listen to the news.
   B Yes, there's one in the kitchen, in the corner by the window
   A Thanks.
2 A I want to post a letter. Have you got any stamps?
   B Sorry, I don't think I've got any. I'll just have a look... No, sorry
   A Oh.
3 A Food's ready!
   B OK, I just want to wash my hands. Have you got any soap?
   A Yes, there's some on the shelf
   B Oh yes, here it is.

Unit 14 good times, bad times

Well, I don't really like January much or February. The weather's cold and wet and it's dark in the evenings – you can go out. And in March it's still cold and windy, I don't like Match much either.

April's a nice month, it's spring, there are flowers everywhere. And I really like May – everything's green, you can sit outside – it's a lovely month, May. I like June, too – the weather's nice, and my birthday's in June too. July and August: I like July and especially August, because I go on holiday in August, and it's hot – I love it. I quite like September because everything starts again – the children go back to school, I start work again, everything's new.
October's all right, I like the colours of the trees, and the weather's sometimes good in October. I don't like November at all – it's dark again, cold, grey... But December's OK, because it's Christmas, I see a lot of friends, have parties – yes, December's a good month.

Unit 15 The next morning

The next morning I went downstairs to the kitchen to have breakfast. My mother was there, and with her was a policeman. The policeman looked at me and asked me, 'Were you awake last night? Did you see anything?' So I told him about the man and about the game we played. The policeman smiled and wrote down what are said in his notebook. Then he asked, 'What was this man like?' So I said that the man was quite tall, he had dark hair, and he had a black jumper and black trousers.
The policeman took a photo from his pocket and gave it to me. 'Is this the man?' he asked. I said, 'Yes it is'. The policeman smiled again. Thank you', he said, and he gave me some chocolate. Then he went away, and my mother gave me breakfast.
   I never saw the man again. But a few weeks later, the policeman came back to our house. He had a large bag with him, and he put it on the kitchen table and opened it. In the bag were all our knives, forks and spoons, our old books, my mother's rings, and our two clocks. 'Your friend gave these back to us,' said the policeman, 'and now we're giving them back to you.'

Unit 16 Other languages

1 I can speak French – I know French from school, and I can speak it quite well. And I speak some Spanish, not very well, but I can speak it. And I know a few words of Italian – *prego, grazie*, things like that. I can say just a few words in Greek - I was on holiday in Greece last year. *Parakalo* means 'please', I remember that. And I know the Arabic for 'yes' – *aiwa* – that's the only word I know in Arabic. And that's all, I think.

2 I can say one or two things in Italian... Numbers, one, two, three... What else? Oh, *arrividerci*, which is 'goodbye', and *prego, grazie* – 'please' and 'thank you' – I think that's all ... Japanese: I know one word – *arigato* – it means 'thank you'. And in Russian I can say *da* and *nyet* – 'yes' and 'no', and *Na zdraviye*, which means 'Cheers!'

Unit 17 Can you remember?

A OK, can you remember the last time you bought some clothes?
B Yes, I think so.
A What did you buy?
B I bought some jeans, some black jeans.
A And where did you buy them?
B It was a shop called the Jean Machine.
A OK, and how much did they cost, these jeans?
B They cost £45.
A OK, now, can you remember last Sunday?
B Yes.
A What was the weather like?
B Oh, it was the sunny - not very hot, but sunny.
A And what did you have for breakfast?
B I had bread, jam, a banana and a glass of fruit juice.
A And what time did you get up, do you remember?
B Yes, because I got up early. I got up at 7 o'clock.
A OK. Now, can you remember the last time you went to a party?
B Yes, that was last Saturday.
A OK, what did you wear?

B What did I wear? I wore my new black jeans, and a shirt, a yellow shirt.
A And what time did you arrive and leave?
B Oh, I arrived at the party at – 8.00, I think. When did I leave? I don't really remember – around 11.00, probably.
A OK, thank you.

Unit 18 Bags of gold

1 OK, you go along the path and up the steps. Climb up the tree to the balcony. Then climb up the ladder to the next balcony. Go along that balcony and across the bridge. Then go up the steps and the bag is at the top

2 You climb up the tree at the corner. Then go along the balcony and up the steps. Go along the next balcony, and go up the second ladder. Then go on up some more steps. And the bag is at the top.

3 Go along the path and up some steps, then climb up a tree. Go along the balcony and down some steps. Then climb down a rope, and the bag is in the window.

4 Climb up the tree at the corner, and then go along the balcony and up some steps. Go along a balcony, and then climb up the long ladder to the next balcony. Go along that balcony and over a birdge. Go along another balcony, and climb down a rope. The bag is in a window.

Unit 19 House rules

A Right, this is the room.
B Oh, very nice.
A Now, there are one or two rules I have to tell you. First of all, you mustn'the smoke in the room. You can smoke on the balcony, but not in the room, please. And you mustn'the cook meals - you can make tea or coffee, that's all right, but no cooking.
B I see, OK. Can I play music?
A Yes, you can play music, but not after 9 o'clock, please.
B What about visitors?
A Well, friends can come and see you, but again, not after 9 o'clock, they must leave by 9 o'clock. And

another thing, you can't have pets, so no dogs or cats, please.
B I've got some pictures. Can I put them on the wall?
A Yes, you can, that's all right, you can put pictures up.
B Good, thank you.
A Oh, one other thing - the window. You must close the window when you go out. Please remember that.
B Yes, all right.

Unit 20 Exercises

1 OK, now stand on one leg, and raise your arms straight above your head. And then look up.
2 Now sit down, cross your legs, and put your hands behind your head
3 Lie down and raise your legs, keep them straight - good. Then raise your arms and head, and put your hands round your legs.
4 Now stand up. Raise your right arm - straight out, that's right - and look along your arm to your fingers.
5 Sit down, and put your legs straight out in front of you. Put your hands behind your back. And raise your legs off the floor-keep them straight ...that's it
6 Now lie down. Keep your left leg and your right arm on the floor. And raise your left arm and your right leg.
7 Stand up. Raise your right leg, so you're just standing on your left leg. Now put your hands round your right leg.
8 Now sit down, cross your legs. And now put your right leg behind your neck. Good. Now put your hands on your head.

Unit 21 Buying things

Conversation 1

A Can I help you?
B Yes, can I see those two rings, please?
A Yes, certainly.
B How much are they?
A Well, this one is £45. And this one is more expensive– it's real gold– £130.
B Oh. I'll have this one for £45, then.

Conversation 2

A Yes?

B I'd like some glasses for fruit juice

A Yes. We've got these ones-they're quite small ...

B Oh yes ...

A Or we've got these -they're a bit bigger.

B Yes, I'd like big ones, I think. I'll have six of these.

A OK. That's 15 then, please.

Conversation 3

A Excuse me

B Yes?

A I'd like an English dictionary

B Yes, well, we've got two, really. There's this one. These are quite good dictionaries, a lot of people buy them. They're £20. Or there's this one, the Cambridge Dictionary-this is a very good dictionary, it really is better than the other one, but of course it's a lot more expensive. It's £45. Hmm, 45 .... OK, I think I'll take the Cambridge Dictionary.

A Hmm, 45 ... OK, I think I'll take the Cambridge Dictionary.

Unit 22 At the weekend

1 Well, I like staying in bed very late – maybe till 10 o'clock or even 11. I like having breakfast in bed and just reading, maybe reading the newspaper or a book. And then I like getting up really slowly, I have a nice hot shower, and I like just doing nothing, really.

2 I like going out at the weekend. So usually I get up early, have a quick shower, have a big breakfast, and then if the weather's nice I like going to the mountains, usually with friends, maybe go walking or climbing, or cycling. And if the weather's bad, I go swimming.

3 I enjoy painting pictures, it's my hobby, so I paint every weekend if I can. I usually get up quite late, but if the weather's nice, I like going out somewhere- by the sea, or by a river maybe. And I take everything I need for painting, and some food-and I paint pictures all day-I love it.

4 Well, I work all week and I have to

get up early, so at the weekend I like getting up late and just doing things around my flat. I like cleaning the flat, cooking meals-friends usually come to see me and we have lunch together. Sometimes I go for a walk, but really I like staying at home.

Unit 23 At the airport

1 Well, I'm going to Japan on business. I'm going for a week, I'm flying to Tokyo, I'm staying there for two days, and then I'm taking the train to Osaka, that's about 300 kilometers west of Tokyo. And I'm staying in Osaka for a few days, and then I'm flying back to England.

2 We're going on holiday to the Canary Islands. We're flying to Tenerife, and then we're taking a bus along the coast, and we're staying in a hotel for two weeks.

3 Well, I'm flying to Italy, I'm going on holiday there. And first I'm staying one night in Rome. Then I'm taking a bus to the south of Italy. I haven't got much money, so I'm probably going to stay at camp-sites.

4 Well, I'm not going anywhere _ actually I'm waiting for my uncle. He's arriving from Switzerland in about half an hour from now. And then I'm taking him back to my flat in London, and he's staying the night with us and then he's going on to Scotland tomorrow.

Unit 24 Three stories

1 Last month I bought a new car, and then I drove into town to go shopping. I left the car, with my coat in it – no money, just my coat – and I went shopping. And white I was at the shops, someone threw a brick through the window and took the coat. I was really upset and very angry – I mean, it was just an old coat but of course the car was new.

2 Well, I was in a plane, we were flying from Singapore to London, and it was a Boeing 747, so a big plane. And it was really bad weather, very windy. And the plane

started going up and down-it felt like a small boat in the middle of the sea. And I was really frightened, I think everyone was frightened. And then suddenly it stopped and it was OK again. But I really thought 'we're going to die'.

3 I remember the first time I went to a rock concert. I was 14, and I went with my sister. It was a U2 concert, and U2 were my favourite band at the time, I knew all their songs-and now we had tickets to go and see them. I was so excited that I didn't sleep at all the night before, didn't want any breakfast. And it was a big concert, about 2,000 people came, but we got there early, and we got right to the front, and they really were good.

Answer key

Unit 1 People and places

A Hello and goodbye

2 - I'm a teacher.
- Oh, really? I'm a student.
3 - Where are you from?
- I'm from London.
4 - Hi! How are you?
- I'm fine, thanks.
5 - Goodbye.
- Goodbye. See you soon.

B To be

1 You are - You're
He is - He's
She is - She's
It is - It's
We are - We're
They are - They're
2 He's from Granada.
It's very big.
She's from London.
They're from New York.
We're teachers here.

C Countries

1 FRANCE   6 JAPAN
2 RUSSIA   7 ITALY
3 SPAIN   8 BRAZIL
4 BRITAIN   9 USA
5 GERMANY
10 ▼AUSTRALIA

Listening: Photos

1 She's a student in London.
2 It's a big flat. It's quite old.
3 He's a teacher and he's from the USA.
4 It's new but it's very small.
5 They're from Australia.

Unit 2 In the family

A One baby, two houses ...

three birds   seven dogs
four babies   eight girls
five cats   nine cars
six boys   ten children

B Numbers 1-20

1 twelve, thirteen, fourteen, fifteen, sixteen, seventeen, eighteen, nineteen, twenty

2 *a* fifteen   *e* twelve
b thirteen   *f* eighteen
c nineteen   *g* eleven
d twenty

C The family

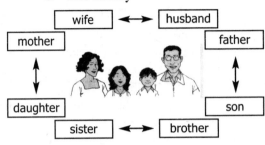

wife ⟷ husband
mother
father
daughter
son
sister ⟷ brother

Listening: Parents and children

1 1 D; 2 B; 3 C; 4 A
2

Study pages A

Check your progress

1 B C D E G P T V
F L M N S X
A J K
Q U
I Y
2 *a* He's   *d* She's
b They're   *e* It's
c I'm
3 *a* has   *c* have ; has
b have   *e* have
4 *5* five   *14* fourteen
7 seven   *18* eighteen
12 twelve   *20* twenty
5 *a* daughter   *d* children
b wife   *e* child
c son

Writing: My friend Maria

2 *Possible answer:*
My brother Ed is six years old.
He has brown hair and grey eyes.
He has a green bike.

Unit 3 To be or not to be?

A I'm not ...

1 I'm not from England.
2 She isn't my wife.
3 You aren't in Class 2A.
4 My friends aren't from the USA.
5 His house isn't big.
6 We aren't teachers.
7 I'm not eighteen.
8 That isn't a dog.

B Yes/no questions

1 Is he English?
2 Are you a doctor?
3 Is she from California?
4 Is this your car?
5 Is it your birthday?
6 Is your name Chris?
7 Are you a policeman?

C Wh- questions

1 How are you?
2 How old is your brother?
3 Who are these people?
4 What is her name?
5 Where is Rome?

Listening: Spell the words

1 ring   5 lamp
2 diamond   6 plant
3 orange   7 mountain
4 apple

Unit 4 Things a round you

A Colours

3 The chair is green.
4 The floor is orange.
5 The hair is grey.
6 The face is yellow.
7 The book is orange.
8 The dress is black.
9 The table is yellow.
10 The wall is blue.
11 The shoes are brown.
12 The door is blue.

B Things

C It's on the desk

1 It's on the chair.
2 They 're under the chair.
3 They're in the bag.
4 It's by the window.
5 They're on the desk.
6 It's behind (by) the door.

Listening: Birthday presents

1 watch, CD
2 pen, dark jumper
3 football , football jumper
4 camera, (one) book
5 computer
6 books, school bag
7 dress, shoes

No number: chair, lamp, ring

Study pages B

Check your progress

1 30 thirty   47 forty-seven
  62 sixty-two   98 ninety-eight
2 a chair   a watch
  an egg   a door
  a ring   an apple
  an umbrella   a mountain
3 Those are nice houses.
  Is that your car?
  This is my son Sam.
4 *a* are; aren't
  b isn't ; are
  c is; are
5 ■ black; □ white; ▨ grey
  Some other colours:
  red; blue; green; yellow; pink;
  orange; brown
6 *a* on   *c* in
  b under   *d* by

Writing: Pictures of people

2 *Possible answers:*
  This is a picture of me with my
  girlfriend. Her name is Carla, and
  she's from the USA. We're (on
  holiday) in Spain.
  This is a picture of me with my
  parents. My farther is 50 and my
  mother is 40. We 're in their
  house in London.

Unit 5 There's ...

A There is and there are

There's a car.
There's a lamp.
There's a chair.
There's a man
There are some (two) birds.
There are some (two) children.
There are some (two) bikes.
There are some (five) books.

C Asking questions

2 Is there a good restaurant in this
  town?
3 How many floors are there in this
  building?
4 How many people are there in
  your family?
5 Is there a university in your town?
6 How many questions are there in
  this exercise?

Listening: Language school

1 There are five classrooms.
2 There is a café for the students.
3 There are 200 students.
4 They have three computers.
5 There are six teachers.

Unit 6 Where you like

A Things in the home

1 phone	9 cooker
2 television	10 shelf
3 sofa	11 radio
4 cupboard	12 plant
5 carpet	13 fridge
6 picture	14 bath
7 clock	15 shower
8 bed	16 mirror

B Where are they?

2 in the living room, on the table by
  the sofa
3 in the bedroom, on the wall (by

---

  the cupboard)
4 in the kitchen, on the fridge
5 in the kitchen, on the shelf
6 in the bathroom, on the wall
7 in the living room, in the corner
  by the door.

C Names and addresses

1 director
2 Morelli; Paul
3 Via Napoli; 011 2394023
4 Edinburgh; Scotland; EH15 3 TW

Listening : Who are you?

NAME:
  Susan Kenedy
ADDRESS:
  23 Abbot Road,
  London SW1A 2JW
TELEPHONE
  0181 622 6460

Study pages C

Check your progress

1 *(you)*	your
(he)	his
(she)	her
(we)	our
(they)	their
(Ronaldo)	Ronaldo's
2 girls	beaches
babies	tables
glasses	carpets

3 *3* the third floor
  6 the six floor
  8 the eighth floor
4 *a* There 's a fridge in the room.
  b There isn't a shower .
  c There aren't any cupboards.
  d There are some plants.
  e There's a TV in the corner.
  f There 's a radio on the shelf.
  g There 's a mirror on the wall.

Writing: Describing places

2 *Possible answers:*
  a There isn't a school, and there's
    only one shop.
  b There isn't a TV, but the bed's
    very comfortable.
  c There are eight bedrooms, and
    there's a swimming pool in the
    garden.

Unit 7 Things people do

A Verbs

2 read   6 watch
3 look   7 talk
4 have   8 go
5 play

B I speak - She speaks

1 speak; speaks; speak
2 has; has; have
3 likes; likes; like
4 play; plays; play

C Adjectives

Across ▶
1 SLOW   3 COLD   4 STRONG
7 WEAR   8 HOT   10 LONG

Down ▼
1 SHORT   2 OLD   5 NEW
6 FAST   8 HIGH   9 LOW

D Positive and negative

1 His parents don't speak Chinese.
2 She doesn't wear beautiful clothes.
3 My mother doesn't like beer.
4 I don't live in Los Angeles.
5 John doesn't go to a good school.
6 My children don't play football.
7 My dog doesn't watch TV.

Listening : I like ...

1 *a* True
   b True
   c False (She doesn't like coffee.)
   d True
   e True
   f False (I don't like dark colours.)
   g False (She's from England.)
   h True
2 *Possible answers:*
   a She likes orange juice.
   b She doesn't like tea.

Unit 8 Food and drink

A Types of food

2 eggs   8 potatoes
3 bread   9 rice
4 pasta   10 beans
5 fruit   11 salad
6 fish   12 meat
7 cheese   13 oil

C Where are they?

1 FORK   6 PLATE
2 SPOON   7 SUGAR
3 SALT   8 BURGER
4 KETCHUP   9 GLASS
5 PERPER   10 KNIFE
Where are they?   ON THE TABLE

Listening; In a restaurant

Conversation 1
The woman has chicken, a green
salad and a Coca Cola.
The man has spaghetti, a green salad
and a bear.
Conversation 2
The man wants fish with potatoes,
vegetables and wine.
The man has fish, tomato salad and a
glass of water.

Study pages D

Check your progress

1 Five o'clock
   (a) quarter past ten (*or* ten fifteen)
   ten to nine (*or* eight fifty) half
   past seven (*or* seven thirty)
2 *(he)*   him   *(we)*   us
   (she)   her   *(they)*   them
3 *a* listen   *d* watch
   b has   *e* goes
   c reads   *f* go
4 *a* eat   *c* doesn't eat
   b don't eat   *d* eats

Writing: Breakfast

2 *Possible answers:*
   I have breakfast at about half past
   six. I usually have bread and
   cheese, and I sometimes have fruit.
   And I drink a glass of orange juice.

   I have breakfast at about half past
   six. I usually have rolls with cheese
   and cold meat, and I sometimes
   have a jam. I drink a cup of coffee.

Unit 9 Do you ...?

A Yes/no questions

1 Do your parents smoke?
2 Does she eat burgers?
3 Does he live in California?
4 Do you have sugar in your coffee?
5 Do your children like pasta?
6 Does she drive a Mercedes?
7 Do your friends live near here?

B Wh-questions

3 What do you study?
4 Where do you study?
6 Where does she work?
7 Where does your brother live?
8 What does he study?
9 Where does he study?

Listening: When are they together?

The man goes to work at 8.00 in the
evening. He gets home at 4.00 in the
morning. He gets up at 12.30. He has
dinner at 7.00.
The woman gets up at 8.00 in the
morning. She gets home at 5.45 in the
evening. She has dinner at 7.00. She
goes to bed at 11.00.
They are together from 5.45 - 8.00 in
the evening.

Unit 10 Things people buy

A Customers

2 - How much is that football?
   - It's £9.50
3 - Can I see that camera?
   - Yes, of course. Here you are.
4 - What size is this jacket?
   - It's size 29.
5 - I'll have five, please.
   - OK. That's £2.50, please.
6 - How much are these jeans?
   - They're £30.
7 - This is a nice one. Only £150.
   - That's too expensive!

B Shops

Some possible answers:
Clothes shop: jeans, jumpers, jackets
Baker: bread, cakes, rolls
Greengrocer: potatoes, apples,
   oranges; vegetables, fruit
Newsagent: newspapers, magazines,
   pens, cigarettes
Chemist: toothpaste, aspirins, tissues,
   sunglasses
Bookshop: books, magazines, maps
Butcher: meat, beef, chicken
Kiosk: cigarettes, pens, lighters,
   ice-creams

C Where is it?

1 in; opposite   4 in; by
2 next to   5 between
3 near

Listening : Shopping

1 Shop: greengrocer
   She buys six oranges, three kilos of potatoes and half a kilo of green beans.
2 Shop: newsagent or kiosk
   She buys an evening paper and a street map.
3 Shop: clothes shop
   She buys a T-shirt.
   She doesn't buy a jumper.

Study pages E

Check your progress

1 He plays tennis on Tuesday afternoon and he plays cards on Wednesday evening. He goes to the shops on Thursday morning and he goes to the cinema on Friday evening.
2 three kilos of potatoes
   half a kilo of sugar
   half a litre of milk
3 *a* What time do you get up?
   b What size are those shoes?
   c Where do your parents live?
   d How much is this radio?
   e What does your brother study?
4 *a* the baker   *c* the bookshop
   b the butcher   *d* the newsagent

Unit 11 What's going on?

A They're listening to the radio

3 He's *having* a shower.
4 He's *reading* a newspaper.
5 They're *playing* table tennis.
6 She's *washing* her hair.
7 He's *making* a (cup of) coffee.
8 She's *writing* a letter.
9 They're *drinking* beer.
10 They're *dancing*.

B Asking questions

2 Where are you staying?
3 What are they watching?
4 What is he drinking?
5 Where are you going?
6 What are they playing?
7 Where is she working?

C Where is he?

2 at school   5 at home
3 at the post office   6 at a party
4 at the cinema   7 at the shops

Listening: On the phone

Ali: Yes. He's watching a football

match. Yes.
Susie: No. She's at the cinema. No.
Sam: Yes. He's doing his homework. No.
Mrs. Lopez: No. She's having lunch. No.

Unit 12 Describing people

A Clothes

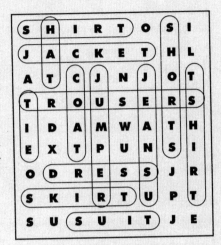

B Jobs

2 He's a waiter. He works in a French restaurant.
3 She's a teacher. She teaches maths.
4 She's a doctor. She works in the hospital.
5 He's a shop assistant. He works in a newsagent.
6 He's a student. He studies French.
7 She's a secretary. She works for British Airways.

Listening: Where are the Browns?

Person E is Mr Brown.
Person M is Mrs Brown.
Person K is Richard.

Study pages F

Check your progress

1 *a* Open; read
   b Close *or* Don't open
   c Don't play
   d Look
   e Don't buy

2 *Some possible answers:*
   I'm wearing a blue jumper.
   I'm writing a sentence.

I'm sitting in my living room.
I'm not wearing a coat.
I'm not playing cards.
I'm not having a shower.
3 taxi driver; singer; shop assistant
   Some other jobs: waiter, doctor, secretary, teacher, engineer
4 *A possible answer:*
   He's a tall man. He has long dark hair. He's wearing shorts, a T-shirt and a hat.

Writing: People doing things

2 *Possible answer:*
   The picture shows a man and a woman. They're having lunch. On the table there is some fish, some bread and a bottle of wine. The man is wearing a skirt and trousers. The woman is wearing a dress.
3 *Possible answer:*
   The picture shows a woman and a man. They're sitting in a train. The woman is wearing a shirt and jumper. The man is wearing a suit and a tie. They're playing cards.

Unit 13 How much?

A Two puzzles

A 2 PHONES
   3 CUPS
   4 RINGS
   5 WATCHES
B 2 COFFEE
   3 WINE
   4 KETCHUP
   5 SOAP
   6 SUGAR
   7 MONEY
   8 WATER

Puzzle A: COUNT nouns
Puzzle B: NON-COUNT nouns

B In (and on) the fridge

b We haven't got many cigarettes.
c We've got lots of beer.
d We haven't got much milk.
e We haven't got any eggs.
f We haven't got much fruit.
g We haven't got any meat.
h We've got lots of cheese.

C How much and How many

2 How many floors
3 How much cheese
4 How much blood
5 How many people
6 How many rooms
7 How much food

Listening: I want ...

1 radio; listen to the news
2 post a letter; stamps
3 wash my hands; soap

Unit 14 Around the year

A Climate and seasons

1 hot; warm
2 wet; dry
3 cool; autumn
4 summer; winter; cold; Spring

B Months

1 January, February, March, April;
  June, July, August; October,
  November, December
2 a August   d January
  b February   e November
  c December

C Weather

2 It's windy.   6 It's humid.
3 It's cold.   7 It's snowing.
4 It's raining.   8 It's cloudy.
5 It's sunny.

Listening: Good times, bad times

1 It's cold and wet; it's dark in the
  evenings; you can't go out.
2 Cold and windy.
3 It's spring; there are flowers
  everywhere.
4 In June.
5 He goes on holiday.
6 Children go back to school; he
  starts work again.
7 He likes the colours of the trees;
  the weather's sometimes good.
8 It's dark, cold and grey.
9 He sees friends; he had parties.

Study pages G

Check your progress

1 a They can swim.
  b They can't ski.
  c Sue can play the piano.
  d Jim can't play the piano.
2 a My brother has got long hair.
  b My parents have got a new car.
  c I haven't got much money.
  d Julia hasn't got a job.
3 three hundred and sixty-five one
  thousand five hundred five hundred
  thousand one milion.
4 A eggs; potatoes
  B food; meat
  C apple; bottle of lemonade
5 a dry; cool
  b spring; winter
  c April; June
  d raining; cloudy

Writing: Birthdays

2 *Possible answer:*

  My birthday is in February. In the
  morning, my parents give me
  presents. Then in the afternoon, I
  usually have a birthday party. All
  my friends come. We play games
  and we have a birthday cake.
  Sometimes we eat ice-cream.

Unit 15 In the past 1

A Verbs in the past

1 ... *gave* me a birthday present ... I
  opened it ... It *was* a cigarette
  lighter ... he *asked* me ... I *said*
  he *said* ... he *took* the lighter ...
  put it in his pocket and *went* out
  of the room.
2 I *was* at home ... My parents *were*
  out ... I *wanted* to see my friends ...
  they *were* out ... I *looked* out of the
  window and *saw* them ... They *had*
  a ball ... we *went* to the park ...
  played football.

C Past descriptions

1 There *were* two people ... They
  were about 50 ... The woman *was*
  quite short and *had* long, grey hair.
  The man *was* very tall and *had* no
  hair ... They *had* a large dog ... The
  dog *had* long grey hair too.

2 It *was* a very good hotel. We *had* a
  lovely room. It *had* a double bed ...
  it also *had* a large balcony ... there
  were three or four chairs ... There
  was a swimming pool... there *were*
  also two very good restaurants. We
  had a lovely time ...

Listening: The next morning

1 False (She was in the kitchen.)
2 True
3 True
4 True
5 True
6 False (He gave him some
  chocolate.)
7 True
8 True
9 False (He came back.)
10 False (He gave them back.)

Unit 16 Around the world

A Places

1 a west   b east   c south
2 A is on a lake
  B is on the coat/on the sea.
  C is in the mountains.
  D is on a river.
3 resort
4 a village   b town
5 islands

B Lauguages

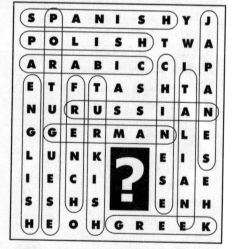

1 French   7 German
2 Russian   8 Italian
3 Portuguese   9 Turkish
4 Spanish   10 Greek
5 Chinese   11 Arabic
6 Polish   12 Japanese

One more language: English

Listening: Other languages

1 True
2 True
3 False (She was on holiday there.)
4 False (She can say a few words.)
5 True
6 True
7 False (He knows one word.)
8 True

Study pages H

Check your progress

1 (the) fourteenth (of) February
  (the) twenty-second (of) August
  (the) twenty-eighth (of) October
  (the) thirty-first (of) December
2 a I wrote them a letter
  b Can you bring me a glass of
    water
  c I gave her some money
3 a in   c in   e in
  b on   d in   f on
4 Yesterday, Paul and Lola had
  breakfast. Then they took the dog to
  the park. Paul bought a newspaper
  and read it. Lola walked through the
  park and played with the dog.
  Then they went home and watched
  TV.
5 a French   d Polish
  b Chinese   e Japanese
  c Russian   f Greek

Writing : and, so, because

2 See Classroom Book.
3 Expected answers:
  a I went to bed early last night
    because I was tired.
  b It was cold, so I went to a clothes
    shop and bought a jumper.
  c My mother was a teacher at my
    school, so we went there
    together every morning.
  d When I was young, we listened
    to the radio because we didn't
    have a TV.

Unit 17 In the past 2

A It's all wrong!

2 They didn't buy a new fridge.
  They bought a camera.
3 They didn't have chicken for
  lunch. They had fish.
4 They didn't play cards. They
  played tennis.
5 They didn't go to a party. They
  went to the cinema.
6 They didn't get home at ten
  o'clock. They got home at 11.30.
7 They didn't watch a football
  match. They watched a film.

B Yes/no questions

2 Was the weather hot?
3 Were the restaurants good?
4 Did you go to the theatre?
5 Did you visit the Empire State
  Building?
6 Did you walk in Central Park?
7 Did you have a good time?

C Wh- questions

2 Where did he sit?
3 What time did she come in?
4 What did he give her?
5 What did she give him?
6 How much money did she give
  him?
7 What time did she leave?

Listening : Can you remember?

1 some jeans; 45 pounds
2 not very hot, but sunny; bread,
  jam, a banana and a glass of fruit
  juice; 7 o'clock
3 black jeans and a yellow shirt;
  8 o'clock; around 11 o'clock

Unit 18 How to get there

A Prepositions

1 past   4 down   7 through
2 out of   5 up   8 along
3 into   6 over   9 across

B Moving around

Across ▶
2 CYCLE 4 DRIVES 6 BUS
9 WALK 10 TAXI 11 TRAIN
Down ▼
1 LEAVE 3 CAR 5 STATION
6 BIKE 7 STOP 8 GET

C Giving directions

1 Go straight along this road.
  There's a chemist on the corner.
  Turn right at the chemist.
  Go past the church.
  The cinema's on the right.
2 Possible answer:
  Go straight along this road.
  There's a bookshop on the
  corner. Turn left at the
  bookshop. Go past the library.
  The swimming pool is on the
  right.

Listening : Bags of gold

1 = G   2 = A   3 = E   4 = F

Study pages I

Check your progress

1 a Yes, I did.
    No, I didn't.
  b Yes, they were.
    No, they weren't.
  c Yes, there is.
    No, there isn't.
2 It's quite slow.
  It isn't very long.
  It's quite cheap.
  She isn't very old.
3 seventeen sixty.
  nineteen ninety-nine.
  two thousand and one.
4 a Did you go to John's birthday
    party?
  b Where was it?
  c What did you wear?
  d Did you enjoy it?
  e What time did you get home?
5 The man goes out of the house,
  along the road, up the steps,
  across the bridge, down the steps
  and into the shop

Writing: Then ...

2 Possible answer:
  At 7 o'clock he left home, walked
  to the station and took a train to
  London. Then he took a bus to his
  office building and went up to the
  10th floor. Then he went into his
  office, sat at his desk and start
  work.

Unit 19 You mustn't do that!

A Must and mustn't

1 You must wash your hair.
  You mustn't wear those shoes
  in the house.
2 You must drink lots of water.
  You mustn't go to school.
  You must stay in bed.
3 You mustn't stay up late.
  You must clean your teeth.
  You must be good!

B Can and can't

Possible answers:

3. You can't wash your hair.
4. You can listen to music.
5. You can write a letter.
6. You can't play a computer game.
7. You can have something to eat.
8. You can't play cards.

C I have to go home

3. You don't have to wear a suit.
4. We don't have to cook a meal.
5. He has to do his homework.
6. You have to do down the stairs.
7. They don't have to stay in a hotel.
8. She doesn't have to walk.

Listening: House rules

One person is smoking ('You mustn't smoke').
They cooked a meal ('You mustn't a meals').
They're playing music ('You mustn't play music after 9 o'clock').
Some friends are there ('Friends mustn't leave by 9 o'clock').
There's a cat ('You can't have pets').

Unit 20 The Body

A Parts of the body

Across ▶

1 NECK 4 NOSE 5 HEAD
8 FINGERS 10 LEGS

Down ▼

2 EYES 3 MOUTH 6 ARMS
7 HANDS 8 FEET 9 EARS

B Using the body

3 She's swimming (in a river).
4 He's climbing (up) a ladder.
5 She's catching a ball.
6 He's throwing a ball.
7 She's walking on her hands.
8 He's standing on his head.
9 He's kicking a (foot) ball.
10 She's jumping over a wall.

C Where did he go?

1 The man ran out of the house.
2 He drove to an airport.
3 He flew across the sea to an island.

4 He rode across the island.
5 He jumped off the bridge into the river.
6 He swam to the rock.
7 He climbed up the rock.

Listening: exercises

1 B   3 C   5 E   7 F
2 A   4 G   6 H   8 D

Study pages J

Check your progress

1 *b* quickly   *e* carefully
  c quietly   *f* slowly
  d well   *g* angrily
2 *a* to; about
  b to; at
  c at; to
3 *Possible answers:*
  a nose, ears, mouth
  b legs, hands, feet
  c throw, catch
  d drive, fly, ride
4 *a* must; don't have to
  b can; mustn't
  c can't; can

Writing: Animals

2 *Possible answer:*
Penguins are usually black and white. They have short legs but large feet. They have very small wings and can't fly, but they can swim very well. They live by the sea and eat fish.

3 *A possible answer (giraffe):*
Giraffes are brown and white, and they are very tall. They have long thin legs and a very long neck, but quite a small head. They eat leaves, and can run very fast.

Unit 21 Good, better, best

A Tourist resorts

2 Merville is colder in winter (than Seatown).
3 Seatown is more expensive.
4 Seatown is more beautiful.
5 Merville has better food.
6 Seatown has cleaner beaches.
7 Merville has better hotels.

B Opposites

2 Chicken is cheaper then beef.
3 Motorbikes are more dangerous than cars
4 English is easier than Russian.
5 Fred is weaker than George.
6 Trains are faster than buses.
7 October is cooler than August.
8 I'm poorer than Bill Gates.

C Who's the tallest?

2 Ben is the shortest.
3 Box B is the biggest.
4 Box D is the smallest.
5 Fred is the oldest.
6 George is the youngest.
7 The Ford is the fastest.
8 The BMW is the slowest.
9 The Ford is the cheapest.
10 The BMW is the most expensive.

Listening: Buying things

1 a ring; cheaper
2 some glasses; fruit juice; bigger
3 a dictionary; better

Unit 22 Free time

B Likes and dislikes

1 She likes staying up late, but she doesn't like getting up early.
2 He enjoys having a bath, but he doesn't enjoy washing his hair.
3 He likes eating, but he doesn't like washing the dishes.
4 She enjoys playing tennis, but she doesn't enjoy watching tennis.

C Sports

go swimming, running, skiing, windsurfing, climbing
play football, golf, volleyball, tennis, basketball

Listening: At the weekend

b 2   *f* 2, 3
c 2   *g* 1, 4
d 4   *h* 2, 4
e 1   *i* 2

Study pages K

Check your progress

1
  a you like to; like to
  b you want to; I have to

2
  a for; to
  b -; to
  c -; for
  d to

3
  a The Toyota is bigger than the Ferrari.
  b The Ferrari is more expensive than the Chevrolet.
  c The Chevrolet is the biggest.
  d The Ferrari is the most expensive.

4 teams or clubs; ground or stadium; stadium; won; lost

Writing: and, but, also

2 *Possible answers:*
I like driving and cycling. I also like going by train and by bus. But I don't like flying.
I like vanilla and strawberry ice-cream, and I quite like chocolate ice-cream, but I don't like coffee ice-cream.

Unit 23 Future plans

A   Going to ...

1 He's going to have a shower.
He's going to have a cup of coffee.
2 They're going to eat ice-creams.
They're going to play in the sand.
3 She's going to drink champagne.
She's going to talk to friends.

B Questions with 'going to'

1 When are United going to win a match?
2 What time is the bus going to arrive?
3 What are you going to wear to the party?
4 How are we going to get home?
5 Where are you going to put it?

Listening: at the airport

1 staying; taking the train
2 going on holiday; staying in a hotel
3 staying one night; taking a bus

4 is arriving; taking him back
  a Staying for a few days
  b A week
  c By bus
  d He hasn't got much money
  e One night.

Unit 24 Feelings

A Suggestions

1	1 ill	4	cold
2	thirsty	5	hot
3	tired	6	hungry

B How do they feel?

1	excited	5	surprised
2	angry	6	happy
3	frightened	7	sad
4	upset		

Listening: Three stories

Story 1: a new car; go shopping; through the window; took her coat; upset and angry.
Story 2: really bad / very windy; go up and down; frightened; it stopped.
Story 3: a rock concert; her sister; excited; didn't sleep; got to the front.

Final review

Positive and negative

1 They aren't rich. (They're not...)
2 I don't drive a Mercedes.
3 My brother doesn't eat meat.
4 We haven't got a dog.
5 There isn't any beer in the fridge.
6 Don't drink that!
7 They didn't go by train.
8 She doesn't have to get up early.

Lists

1 husband; daughter
2 living room, kitchen, (hall, toilet)
3 fork; pepper
4 *Four of:* greengrocer, newsagent, chemist, baker, butcher, (bank)
5 *Five of:* skirt, T-shirt, blouse, jeans, tie, suit, shoes, coat, jacket
6 February, April
7 north, west
8 *Three of:* taxi, bus, train, bike (bicycle), (ferry) boat
9 *Five of:* hands, fingers, mouth, nose, eyes, ears, body, legs, feed

10 *Three of:* surprised, angry, excited, frightened, upset

Verbs

1 live; is; teaches; works
2 has; is wearing; is standing; is looking
3 got; went; bought; sat; hat; read; smoked

Numbers and words

1 three hundred and eighteen
2 one million seven hundred thousand
3 a quarter to twelve or eleven forty-five
4 (the) twenty-second (of) November
5 nineteen seventy-seven

Questions

1 Where are you from?
2 Is there a TV in your bedroom?
3 How many students are there in the class?
4 What time / when does she start work?
5 Where are they staying?
6 How much rice is there?
7 When did he arrive?
8 Were you at home yesterday?
9 Can she speak French?
10 What are you going to wear?

Conversations

1 Can (Could); Here (There)
2 there; mind
3 Hurry; moment *or* minute
4 Would; thanks
5 does; idea

Prepositions

1 by *or* next to; on; in; under; between
2 on; at; in
3 in; on

Nouns, adjectives and verbs

1 Spanish; Turkish; Russian; Arabic
2 low; strong
    difficult; slow
3 highest; longest; shorter; bigger
4 rode; jumped; swam; climbed; gave

Infinitive	Past tense
be	was/were
bring	brought
build	built
buy	bought
can	could
catch	caught
come	came
cost	cost
do	did
drink	drank
drive	drove
eat	ate
fall	fell
feel	felt
find	found
fly	flew
get	got
give	gave
go	went
have	had
keep	kept
know	knew
leave	left
lose	lost
make	made
pay	paid
put	put
read	read
ride	rode
run	ran
say	said
see	saw
sell	sold
send	sent
sing	sang
sit	sat
sleep	slept
speak	spoke
spend	spent
stand	stood
swim	swam
take	took
tell	told
think	thought
throw	threw
wake	woke
wear	wore
win	won
write	wrote

Phonetic symbols

Vowels

Symbol	Example
/i:/	tree /tri:/
/i/	many /'meni/
/ɪ/	six /sɪks/
/e/	bed /bed/
/æ/	black /blæk/
/ʌ/	much /mʌtʃ/
/ɑ:/	car /kɑ:/
/ɒ/	hot /hɒt/
/ɔ:/	sport /spɔ:t/
/ʊ/	look /lʊk/
/u:/	spoon /spu:n/
/ɜ:/	girl /gɜ:l/
/ə/	about /ə'baʊt/
	water /'wɔ:tə/
/eɪ/	play /pleɪ/
/aɪ/	time /taɪm/
/ɔɪ/	boy /bɔɪ/
/əʊ/	home /həʊm/
/aʊ/	out /aʊt/
/ɪə/	here /hɪə/
/eə/	there /ðeə/

Consonants

Symbol	Example
/p/	pen /pen/
/b/	book /bʊk/
/t/	take /teɪk/
/d/	dog /dɒg/
/k/	cat /kæt/
/g/	go /gəʊ/
/tʃ/	church /tʃɜ:tʃ/
/dʒ/	jumper /'dʒʌmpə/
/f/	for /fɔ:/
/v/	love /lʌv/
/θ/	think /θiŋk/
/ð/	this /ðɪs/
/s/	six /sɪks/
/z/	is /ɪz/
/ʃ/	shop /ʃɒp/
/ʒ/	leisure /'leʒə/
/h/	house /haʊs/
/m/	make /meɪk/
/n/	name /neɪm/
/ŋ/	bring /brɪŋ/
/l/	look /lʊk/
/r/	road /rəʊd/
/j/	young /jʌŋ/
/w/	wear /weə/

Stress

Dictionaries usually show stress by a mark (/'/) before the stressed syllable: teacher /'ti:tʃə/; about /ə'baʊt/; America /ə'merɪkə/.

Acknowledgements

The authors and publishers are grateful to the following illustrators and photographer:

Illustrators: Chris Brown: pp.11, 13 *b*, 21, 27, 43, 70 *t*, 80, 86 *b*; Rachel Deacon: pp.18 *t*, 22; Karen Donnelly: pp. 10 *t*, 13 *t*, 17 *b*, 31, 33, 46 *b*, 60 I, 62 *t*, 69, 70 *b*, 81 *b*, 86 *t*; Nick Duffy: pp. 19 *b*, 20 *tl*, 32 *bl*, 40, 42 *b*, 44 *bl*, 46 *t*, 49, 50 *l*, 58, 61 *bl*, 66, 73, 74 *ml*; Nadime Faye-James: p. 12; Phil Healey: pp. 10 *b*, 20 *ml*, 25 *bl*, 28, 35, 44 *tl*, 52, 55, 60 *b*, 64, 72, 79; Rosalind Hudson: p. 53 *ml*; Amanda McPhail: pp. 36 I, 38 *tl*, 41, 45, 67, 76 *tl*, 78; David Mitcheson: pp. 19 *t*, 20 *bl*, 24, 26 *l*, 36 *b*, 65 *bl*, 81 *t*; Desmond Nicholas:p. 30 *t*; Pantelis Palios: pp. 16, 30 *b*, 53 *tr*, 59, 65 *tr*, 68 *m*, 76 *b*; Tracy Rich: pp. 18 *b*, 42 *t*; Jamie Sneddon: pp. 17 *t*, 25 *tr*, 32 *tl*, 33, 37, 38 *br*, 54, 61 *tr*, 70 *m*, 71, 79; Kath Walker: pp. 14, 20 *r*, 26 *r*, 32 *r*, 38 *tr*, 44 *r*, 50 I, 56, 62 *tr*, 68 *r*, 74 *r*.

Photographer: Jules Selmes: pp. 15, 29, 34, 39, 51

t = top   *m* = middle   *b* = bottom   *r* = right   l = left

Cover design by Dunne & Scully.

Design, production and repro handled by Gecko Limited, Bicester, Oxon.

Sound recordings by Martin Williamson, Prolingua Productions at studio AVP.

Freelance editorial work by Meredith Levy.